Temper Your Child's Tantrums

*How firm, loving discipline
will lead to a more peaceful home*

Dr. James
DOBSON

TYNDALE
MOMENTUM™

*The nonfiction imprint of
Tyndale House Publishers, Inc.*

Visit Tyndale online at www.tyndale.com.

Visit Tyndale Momentum online at www.tyndalemomentum.com.

TYNDALE, Tyndale Momentum, and Tyndale's quill logo are registered trademarks of Tyndale House Publishers, Inc. The Tyndale Momentum logo is a trademark of Tyndale House Publishers, Inc. Tyndale Momentum is the nonfiction imprint of Tyndale House Publishers, Inc., Carol Stream, Illinois.

Temper Your Child's Tantrums: How Firm, Loving Discipline Will Lead to a More Peaceful Home

Designed by Ron Kaufmann

Unless otherwise indicated, all Scripture quotations are taken from *The Living Bible,* copyright © 1971 by Tyndale House Foundation. Used by permission of Tyndale House Publishers, Inc., Carol Stream, Illinois 60188. All rights reserved.

Scripture quotations marked KJV are taken from the *Holy Bible,* King James Version.

Scripture verses marked *Phillips* are taken from *The New Testament in Modern English* by J. B. Phillips, copyright © J. B. Phillips, 1958, 1959, 1960, 1972. All rights reserved.

ISBN 978-1-4143-5952-6. Repackage first published in 2014. Previously published under ISBN 978-0-8423-6994-7.

For information about special discounts for bulk purchases, please contact Tyndale House Publishers at csresponse@tyndale.com or call 800-323-9400.

Library of Congress Cataloging-in-Publication Data

Dobson, James C., date.
   Temper your child's tantrums : how firm, loving discipline will lead to a more peaceful home / Dr. James Dobson.
      pages cm
   Includes bibliographical references.
   ISBN 978-1-4143-5952-6 (mass paper)
1. Discipline of children. 2. Child rearing. I. Title.
   HQ770.4.D62 2014
   649'.1—dc23   2013043597

Printed in the United States of America

23   22
7   6   5

CONTENTS

Every Parent Needs a Game Plan

A woman with seven rambunctious children boarded a Los Angeles bus and sat in the seat behind me. Her hair was a mess, and the gaunt look on her face revealed a state of utter exhaustion. As she stumbled past me with her wiggling tribe, I asked, "Do all these children belong to you, or is this some kind of picnic?"

She looked at me through sunken eyes and said, "They're all mine, and believe me, it's *no* picnic!"

I smiled to myself, understanding fully what she meant. Small children have an uncanny ability to unravel an adult nervous system. They can be noisy and they make incredible messes and they bicker with one another and their noses drip and they throw temper tantrums and they have more energy in their fat little fingers than Mama has in her entire weary body.

PARENTHOOD:
MORE DIFFICULT THAN IT LOOKS

There's no doubt about it: children are expensive little people. To raise them properly will require the *very best* that you can give of your time, effort, and financial resources.

However, to those who have never experienced parenthood, the job may appear ridiculously simple. Such people remind me of a man watching the game of golf for the first time, thinking, "That looks easy. All you have to do is hit that little white ball out there in the direction of the flag." He then steps up to the tee, draws back his club, and dribbles the "little white ball" about nine feet to the left. Accordingly, I should warn those who have not yet assumed the responsibilities of parenthood: the game of raising kids is more difficult than it looks.

So parenthood is costly and complex. Am I suggesting, then, that newly married couples should remain childless?

Certainly not! The family that loves children and wants to experience the thrill of procreation should not be frightened by the challenge of parenthood. Speaking from my own perspective as a father, there have been no greater moments in my life than when I gazed into the eyes of my infant daughter, and five years later, my son.

What could be more exciting than seeing those tiny human beings begin to blossom and grow and learn and love?

And what reward could be more meaningful than having my little boy or girl climb onto my lap as I sit by the fire, hug my neck and whisper, "I love you, Dad."

Oh, yes, *children are expensive, but they're worth the price.* Besides, nothing worth having comes cheap.

IN SEARCH OF A COURSE

Many of the frustrations of parenthood occur because we have no well-designed model or "game plan" to follow in response to the inevitable circumstances that develop. Then when the routine, predictable problems occur, we try to muddle through by random trial and error.

Parents who follow this course remind me of a friend who flew his single-engine airplane toward a small country airport. He arrived as the sun was dropping behind a mountain at the close of the day, and by the time he had maneuvered his plane into position to land, he could not see the hazy field below. He had no lights on his plane, and no one was on duty at the airport.

He circled the runway for another attempt to land, but the darkness had then become even more impenetrable. For two hours he flew his plane around and around in the blackness of night, knowing that he faced certain death when his fuel was expended.

Then, as panic gripped him, a miracle occurred. Someone on the ground heard the continuing drone of his engine and realized his predicament. That merciful man drove his car back and forth on the runway to show my friend the location of the airstrip, and then let his lights cast their beam from the far end while the plane landed.

I think of that story whenever I am descending at night in a commercial airliner. As I look ahead, I can see the green lights bordering the runway which tell the captain where to direct the plane. If he stays between those lighted boundaries, all will be well. There is safety in the illuminated zone, but disaster lies to the left or right.

Isn't that what we need as parents? There should be clearly marked boundaries that tell us where to steer the family ship. We require some guiding *principles* that will help us raise our children in safety and health.

HOPE FOR THE STRONG-WILLED CHILD

My purpose in writing this book is to provide some of those understandings that will contribute to competent parenthood. We will deal particularly with the subject of discipline as it relates to the "strong-willed child." Most parents have at least one such youngster who seems to be born with a clear idea of how he wants the world to be operated and an intolerance for those who disagree. Even in infancy, he fairly bristles when his dinner is late and he insists that someone hold him during every waking hour. Later, during toddlerhood, he declares total war on all forms of authority, at home or abroad, and his greatest thrill comes from drawing on the walls and flushing kitties down the toilet. His parents are often guilt-ridden and frustrated people who wonder where they've gone wrong and why their home life is so different than they were led to expect.

We'll be investigating this self-propelled youngster during his progression through childhood, including infancy, toddlerhood, elementary school years, and pre-adolescence. It is my firm conviction that the strong-willed child usually possesses more creative potential and strength of character than his compliant siblings, provided his parents can help him channel his impulses and gain control of his rampaging will. My writings are dedicated to this purpose.

In short, this book is designed to provide *practical* advice and suggestions to parents who may be reacting to these more difficult challenges without design or forethought. And if I've been successful, this discourse may offer a lighted runway to pilots who circle in the darkness above.

1

Battle of the Wills

The Dobson household consists of a mother and father, a boy and a girl, one hamster, a parakeet, one lonely goldfish, and two hopelessly neurotic cats. We all live together in relative harmony with a minimum of conflict and strife.

But there is another member of our "family" who is less congenial and cooperative. He is a stubborn twelve-pound dachshund named Sigmund Freud (Siggie), who honestly believes he owns the place. All dachshunds tend to be somewhat independent, I'm told, but Siggie is a confirmed revolutionary. He's not vicious or mean; he just wants to run things—and the two of us have been engaged in a power struggle for the past twelve years.

Siggie is not only stubborn, but he doesn't pull his own weight in the family. He won't bring in the newspaper on cold mornings; he refuses to "chase a ball" for the children; he doesn't keep the gophers out of the garden; and he can't do any of the usual tricks that most cultured dogs perform. Alas, Siggie has refused to participate in any of the self-improvement programs I have initiated on his behalf. He is content just to trot through life, watering and sniffing and stopping to smell the roses.

Furthermore, Sigmund is not even a good watchdog. This suspicion was confirmed the night we were visited by a prowler who had entered our backyard at three o'clock in the morning. I suddenly awoke from a deep sleep, got out of bed, and felt my way through the house without turning on the lights. I knew someone was on the patio and Siggie knew it, too, because the little coward was crouched behind me!

After listening to the thumping of my heart for a few minutes, I reached out to take hold of the rear doorknob. At that moment, the backyard gate quietly opened and closed. Someone had been standing three feet from me, and that "someone" was now tinkering in my garage.

Siggie and I held a little conversation in the darkness and decided that he should be the one to investigate the disturbance. I opened the back door and told my dog to "attack!" But Siggie just *had* one! He stood there throbbing and shaking so badly that I couldn't even push him out the back door. In the noise and confusion that ensued, the intruder escaped (which pleased both dog *and* man).

WHO'S BOSS?

Please don't misunderstand me. Siggie is a member of our family and we love him dearly. And despite his anarchistic nature, I have finally taught him to obey a few simple commands. However, we had some classic battles before he reluctantly yielded to my authority.

The greatest confrontation occurred a few years ago when I had been in Miami for a three-day conference. I returned to observe that Siggie had become boss of the house while I was gone. But I didn't realize until later that evening just how strongly he felt about his new position as Captain.

At eleven o'clock that night, I told Siggie to go get into his bed, which is a permanent enclosure in the family room. For six years I had given him that order at the end of each day, and for six years Siggie had obeyed.

On this occasion, however, he refused to budge. You see, he was in the bathroom, seated comfortably on the furry lid of the toilet seat. That is his favorite spot in the house, because it allows him to bask in the warmth of a nearby electric heater. (Incidentally, Siggie had to learn the hard way that it is extremely important that the lid be *down* before he leaves the ground. I'll never forget the night he learned that lesson. He came thundering in from the cold, sailed through the air—and nearly drowned before I could get him out.)

When I told Sigmund to leave his warm seat and go to bed, he flattened his ears and slowly turned his head toward me. He deliberately braced himself by placing one paw on the edge of the furry lid, then hunched his shoulders, raised his lips to reveal the molars on both sides, and uttered his most threatening growl. That was Siggie's way of saying, "Get lost!"

I had seen this defiant mood before, and knew there was only one way to deal with it. The *only* way to make Siggie obey is to threaten him with destruction. Nothing else works. I turned and went to my closet and got a small belt to help me "reason" with Mr. Freud. My wife, who was watching this drama unfold, tells me that as soon as I left the room, Siggie jumped from his perch and looked down the hall to see where I had gone. Then he got behind her and growled.

When I returned, I held up the belt and again told my angry dog to go get into his bed. He stood his ground, so I gave him a firm swat across the rear end, and he tried to bite the belt. I hit him again and he tried to bite *me*.

What developed next is impossible to describe. That tiny dog and I had the most vicious fight ever staged between man and beast. I fought him up one wall and down the other, with both of us scratching and clawing and growling and swinging the belt. I am embarrassed by the memory of the entire scene. Inch by inch I moved him toward the family room and his bed. As a final desperate maneuver, Siggie jumped up on the couch and backed into the corner for one last snarling stand. I eventually got him to bed, but only because I outweighed him 200 to 12!

The following night I expected another siege of combat at Siggie's bedtime. To my surprise, however, he accepted my command without debate or complaint, and simply trotted toward the family room in perfect submission. In fact, that fight occurred more than four years ago, and from that time to this, Siggie has never made another "go for broke" stand.

It is clear to me now that Siggie was saying in his canine way, "I don't think you're tough enough to make me obey." Perhaps I seem to be humanizing the behavior of a dog, but I think not. Veterinarians will confirm that some breeds of dogs, notably dachshunds and shepherds, will not accept the leadership of their masters until human authority has stood the test of fire and proved itself worthy.

But this is not a book about the discipline of dogs; there is an important moral to my story that is highly relevant to the world of children. *Just as surely as a dog will occasionally challenge the authority of his leaders, so will a little child— only more so.*

This is no minor observation, for it represents a characteristic of human nature which is rarely recognized (or admitted) by the "experts" who write books on the subject of discipline. I have yet to find a text for parents or teachers that acknowledges the struggle—the exhausting confrontation of wills—most parents and teachers experience regularly with their children. Adult leadership is rarely accepted unchallenged by the next generation; it must be "tested" and found worthy of allegiance by the youngsters who are asked to yield and submit to its direction.

5

WHY CHILDREN CHALLENGE AUTHORITY

Why are children so pugnacious? Everyone knows that they are lovers of justice and law and order and secure boundaries. The writer of the book of Hebrews in the Bible even said that an undisciplined child feels like an illegitimate son or daughter, not even belonging to his family. Why, then, can't parents resolve all conflicts by the use of quiet discussions and explanations and gentle pats on the head?

The answer is found in the curious value system of children that respects strength and courage (when combined with love). What better explanation can be given for the popularity of the mythical Superman and Captain Marvel and Wonder Woman in the folklore of children? Why else do children proclaim, "My dad can beat up your dad!"? (One child replied to that statement, "That's nothing. My *mom* can beat up my dad, too!")

A HIERARCHY OF STRENGTH

You see, boys and girls care about the issue of "who's toughest." Whenever a youngster moves into a new neighborhood or a new school district, he usually has to fight (either verbally or physically) to establish himself in the hierarchy of strength. Anyone who understands children knows that there is a "top dog" in every group, and there is a poor little defeated pup at the bottom of the heap. And every child between those extremes knows where he stands in relation to the others.

Recently my wife and I had an opportunity to observe this social hierarchy in action. We invited the fourteen girls in our daughter's fifth-grade class to our home for a slumber party. It was a noble gesture, but I can tell you with sincerity that we will never do that again. It was an exhausting and sleepless night of giggling and wiggling and jumping and bumping. But it was also a very interesting evening, from a social point of view.

The girls began arriving at five o'clock on Friday night, and their parents returned to pick them up at eleven o'clock Saturday morning. I met most of them for the first time that weekend, yet during those seventeen hours together, I was able to identify every child's position in the hierarchy of respect and strength.

There was one queen bee who was boss of the crowd. Everyone wanted to do what she suggested, and her jokes brought raucous laughter. Then a few degrees below her was the number two princess, followed by three, four, and five. At the bottom of the list was a harassed little girl who was alienated and rejected by the entire herd. Her jokes were as clever (I thought) as those of the leader, yet no one laughed when she clowned. Her suggestions of a game or event were immediately condemned as stupid and foolish. I found myself defending this isolated girl because of the injustice of her situation. Unfortunately, there is a similar outcast or loser in every group of three or more kids (of either sex). Such is the nature of childhood.

> **Children want to know how "tough" their leaders are.**

7

This respect for strength and courage also makes children want to know how "tough" their leaders are. They will occasionally disobey parental instructions for the precise purpose of testing the determination of those in charge. Thus, whether you are a parent or grandparent or Boy Scout leader or bus driver or Brownie leader or schoolteacher, I can guarantee that sooner or later, one of the children under your authority will clench his little fist and challenge your leadership. Like Siggie at bedtime, he will convey this message by his disobedient manner: "I don't think you are tough enough to make me do what you say."

GAMES CHILDREN PLAY

This defiant game, called Challenge the Chief, can be played with surprising skill by very young children. Recently a father told me of taking his three-year-old daughter to a basketball game. The child was, of course, interested in everything in the gym except the athletic contest.

The father permitted her to roam free and climb on the bleachers, but he set up definite limits regarding how far she could stray. He took her by the hand and walked with her to a stripe painted on the gym floor. "You can play all around the building, Janie, but don't go past this line," he instructed her.

He had no sooner returned to his seat than the toddler scurried in the direction of the forbidden territory. She stopped at the border for a moment, then flashed a grin over her shoulder to her father, and deliberately placed one foot over the line as if to say, "Whacha gonna do about it?"

Virtually every parent the world over has been asked the same question at one time or another.

The entire human race is afflicted with the same tendency toward willful defiance that this three-year-old exhibited. Her behavior in the gym is not so different from the folly of Adam and Eve in the Garden of Eden. God had told them they could eat *anything* in the Garden except the forbidden fruit ("do not go past this line"). Yet they challenged the authority of the Almighty by deliberately disobeying His commandment. Perhaps this tendency toward self-will is the essence of "original sin" which has infiltrated the human family. It certainly explains why I place such stress on the proper response to willful defiance during childhood, for that rebellion can plant the seeds of personal disaster. The thorny weed which it produces may grow into a tangled briar patch during the troubled days of adolescence.

When a parent refuses to accept his child's defiant challenge, something changes in their relationship. The youngster begins to look at his mother and father with disrespect; they are unworthy of his allegiance. More important, he wonders why they would let him do such harmful things if they really loved him.

> **The ultimate paradox of childhood: boys and girls want to be led by their parents, but insist that their mothers and fathers earn the right to lead them.**

TWO KINDS OF KIDS

I have been watching infants and toddlers during recent years, and have become absolutely convinced that at the moment of birth there exists in children an inborn temperament which will play a role throughout life.

Though I would have denied the fact fifteen years ago, I am now certain that the personalities of newborns vary tremendously, even before parental influence is exercised. Every mother of two or more children will affirm that each of her infants had a different personality—a different "feel"—beginning with the first time they were held.

Numerous authorities in the field of child development now agree that these complex little creatures called babies are far from "blank slates" when they enter the world. One important study by Chess, Thomas, and Birch revealed nine kinds of behaviors in which babies differ from one another. These differences tend to persist into later life and include level of activity, responsiveness, distractibility, and moodiness, among others.

Another newborn characteristic (not mentioned by Chess) relates to a feature that can be called "strength of the will."

1. *The compliant child.* Some children seem to be born with an easygoing, compliant attitude toward external authority. As infants they don't cry very often and they sleep through the night from the second week and they goo at the grandparents and they smile while being diapered and

they're very patient when dinner is overdue. And, of course, they never spit up on the way to church.

During later childhood, they love to keep their rooms clean and they especially like to do their homework and they can entertain themselves for hours. There aren't many of these supercompliant children, I'm afraid, but they are known to exist in some households (not my own).

2. *The strong-willed child.* Just as surely as some children are naturally compliant, there are others who seem to be defiant upon exit from the womb. They come into the world smoking a cigar and yelling about the temperature in the delivery room and the incompetence of the nursing staff and the way things are run by the administrator of the hospital. They expect meals to be served the instant they are ordered, and they demand every moment of mother's time. As the months unfold, their expression of willfulness becomes even more apparent, the winds reaching hurricane force during toddlerhood.

In thinking about these compliant and defiant characteristics of children, I sought an illustration to explain the vastly differing thrust of human temperaments. I found an appropriate analogy in a supermarket shortly thereafter.

Imagine yourself in a grocery store, pushing a wire cart up the aisle. You give the basket a small shove and it glides at least nine feet out in front, and then comes to a gradual stop. You walk along, happily tossing in the soup and ketchup bottles and loaves of bread. Marketing is such an easy task, for even when the cart is burdened with goods, it can be directed with one finger.

But buying groceries is not always so blissful. On other occasions, you select a shopping cart that ominously awaits your arrival at the front of the market. When you push the stupid thing forward, it tears off to the left and knocks over a stack of bottles. Refusing to be outmuscled by an empty cart, you throw all of your weight behind the handle, fighting desperately to keep the ship on course. It seems to have a mind of its own as it darts toward the eggs and careens back in the direction of the milk and almost crushes a terrified grandmother in green tennis shoes. You are trying to do the same shopping assignment that you accomplished with ease the week before, but the job feels more like combat duty today. You are exhausted by the time you herd the rebellious cart toward the checkout stand.

What is the difference between the two shopping baskets? Obviously, one has straight, well-oiled wheels which go where they are guided. The other has crooked, bent wheels that refuse to yield.

Do you recognize how this illustration relates to children? We might as well face it, some kids have "crooked wheels"! They do not want to go where they are led, for their own inclinations would take them in other directions.

Furthermore, the mother who is "pushing the cart" must expend seven times the energy to make it move, compared with the parent of a child with "straight, well-oiled wheels." (Only mothers of strong-willed children will *fully* comprehend the meaning of this illustration.)

IS YOUR CHILD TYPICAL?

But how does the "typical" or "average" child respond? My original assumption was that children in the Western world probably represented a "normal" or bell-shaped curve with regard to strength of the will. In other words, I presumed there were a few very compliant kids and an equally small number who were defiant, but the great majority of youngsters were likely to fall somewhere near the middle of the distribution.

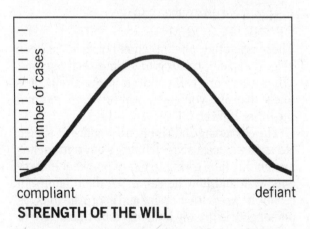

STRENGTH OF THE WILL

However, having talked to at least 25,000 harried parents, I'm convinced that my supposition was wrong. The true distribution probably is depicted in the following chart. (Don't take this observation too literally, for perhaps it only *seems* that the majority of toddlers are trying to conquer the world.)

13

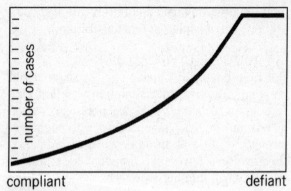

number of cases

compliant   defiant

STRENGTH OF THE WILL

SIBLINGS: OPPOSITE ENDS
OF THE SPECTRUM

There is another phenomenon I have never been able to explain, relating to sibling relationships. When there are two children in the family, it is likely that one youngster will be *compliant* and the other *defiant*.

The easygoing child is often a genuine charmer. He smiles at least sixteen hours a day and spends most of his time trying to figure out what his parents want and how he can make them happy. In reality, he *needs* their praise and approval; thus his personality is greatly influenced by this desire to gain their affection and recognition.

The second child is approaching life from the opposite vantage point. He is sliding all four brakes and trying to gain control of the family steering mechanism. Can you see how these differences in temperament lay the foundation for serious sibling rivalry and resentment?

14

The defiant child faces constant discipline and hears many threats and finger-wagging lectures, while his angelic brother, little Goody-Two-Shoes, polishes his halo and soaks up the warmth of parental approval. The two are pitted against each other by the nature of their divergent personalities, and may spend a lifetime scratching and clawing one another.

DOS AND DON'TS FOR
BATTLE-WORN PARENTS

There are several other observations that may be helpful to the parents of a strong-willed child.

1. Do acknowledge the guilt and anxiety that you, as a conscientious parent, commonly feel. You are engaged in an all-out tug-of-war that naturally leaves you frustrated and fatigued. No one told you that parenthood would be this difficult!

2. Don't blame yourself for the tension that arises between you and your strong-willed child. Many people plan to be such loving and effective parents, reading fairy stories to their pajama-clad angels by the fireplace. The difference between life as it is and life as it ought to be can be a frightening and distressing bit of reality.

3. Don't be intimidated by the parents of compliant children who don't understand your difficulties with your defiant youngsters.

4. Do ignore comments that imply, "If you would raise your kids the way I do it, you wouldn't be having those awful problems." Statements like these only intensify guilt and anxiety.

5. Do take courage in the fact that the willful

child can be difficult to control even when his parents handle him with great skill and dedication. It may take several years to bring him to a point of relative obedience and cooperation within the family unit.

6. Don't try to complete the transformation overnight. While this training program is in progress, it is important not to panic.

7. Do treat your child with sincere love and dignity, but require him to follow your leadership.

8. Do choose carefully the matters which are worthy of confrontation, then accept his challenge on those issues and *win* decisively.

9. Do reward every positive, cooperative gesture your child makes by offering your attention, affection, and verbal praise.

THE KEY TO YOUR CHILD'S POTENTIAL

The most urgent advice I can give the parents of an assertive, independent child concerns the importance of beginning to shape his will during the *early* years.

I honestly believe, though the assumption is difficult to prove, that the defiant youngster is in a "high risk" category for antisocial behavior later in life. He is more likely to challenge his teachers in school and question the values he has been taught and shake his fist in the faces of those who would lead him. I believe he is more inclined toward sexual promiscuity and drug abuse and academic difficulties.

This is not an inevitable prediction, of course, because the complexities of the human personality make it impossible to forecast behavior with complete accuracy. I must also stress that the overall picture is not negative. It would appear that the strong-willed child may possess more character and have greater potential for a productive life than his compliant counterpart.

However, the realization of that potential may depend on a firm but loving early home environment. Thus, I repeat my admonition: *Begin shaping the will of that child while he is in toddlerhood.* (Notice that I did not say *crush* the will, or destroy it, or snuff it out. The "how to" of this recommendation will provide the subject matter of subsequent chapters.)

To Spank—or Not to Spank?

The young mother of a defiant three-year-old girl recently approached me in Kansas City to thank me for my books and tapes. She told me that a few months earlier her little daughter had become increasingly defiant and had managed to "buffalo" her frustrated mom and dad. They knew they were being manipulated but couldn't seem to regain control.

Then one day they happened to see a copy of my first book, *Dare to Discipline*, on sale in a local bookstore. They bought the book and learned therein that it is appropriate to spank a child under certain well-defined circumstances. My recommendations made sense to these harassed parents, who promptly spanked their sassy daughter the next time she gave them reason to do so.

But the little girl was just bright enough to figure out where they had picked up that new idea. When the mother awoke the next morning, she found her copy of *Dare to Discipline* floating in the toilet! That darling little girl had done her best to send my writings to the sewer, where they belonged, in her opinion. I suppose that is the strongest editorial comment I've received on any of my literature!

This incident with the toddler was not an isolated case. Another child selected my book from an entire shelf of possibilities and threw it in the fireplace. I could easily become paranoid about these hostilities. Dr. Benjamin Spock is loved by millions of children who have grown up under his influence, but I am apparently resented by an entire generation of kids who would like to catch me in a blind alley on some cloudy night.

Without a doubt, children are aware of the contest of wills between generations, and that is precisely why the parental response is so important. When a child behaves in ways that are disrespectful or harmful to himself or others, his hidden purpose is often to verify the stability of the boundaries.

This testing has much the same function as a policeman who turns doorknobs at places of business after dark. Though he tries to open doors, he hopes they are locked and secure.

Likewise, a child who assaults the loving authority of his parents is greatly reassured when their leadership holds firm and confident. He finds his greatest security in a structured environment where the rights of other people (and his own) are protected by definite boundaries.

Our objective, then, is to *shape the will* during the early years of childhood. But how is that to be accomplished? I have talked to hundreds of parents who recognize the validity of the principle but have no idea how it can be implemented in their homes. Consequently, the remainder of this chapter has been devoted to specific suggestions and recommendations. We will begin with six broad guidelines which are paraphrased from my previous writings, followed by practical examples at each age level.

HOW TO SHAPE A CHILD'S WILL
1. *Define the boundaries before they are enforced.*

The most important step in any disciplinary procedure is to establish reasonable expectations and boundaries *in advance*. The child should know what is and what is not acceptable behavior *before* he is held responsible for those rules. This precondition will eliminate the overwhelming sense of injustice that a youngster feels when he is slapped or punished for his accidents, mistakes, and blunders. If you haven't defined it—don't enforce it!

2. *When defiantly challenged, respond with confident decisiveness.*

Once a child understands what is expected, he should then be held accountable for behaving accordingly. That sounds easy, but as we have seen, most children will assault the authority of their elders and challenge their right to lead. In a moment of rebellion, a little child will consider his parents' wishes and defiantly choose to disobey. Like a military general before a battle, he will calculate the potential risks, marshal his forces and attack the enemy with guns blazing.

When that nose-to-nose confrontation occurs between generations, it is *extremely* important for the adult to win decisively and confidently. The child has made it clear that he's looking for a fight, and his parents would be wise not to disappoint him!

> **If you haven't defined it—don't enforce it!**

Nothing is more destructive to parental leadership than for a mother or father to disintegrate during that struggle. When the parent consistently loses those battles, resorting to tears and screaming and other evidence of frustration, some dramatic changes take place in the way they are "seen" by their children. Instead of being secure and confident leaders, the parents become spineless jellyfish who are unworthy of respect or allegiance.

3. *Distinguish between willful defiance and childish irresponsibility.*

A child should not be spanked for behavior that is not willfully defiant. When he forgets to feed the dog or make his bed or take out the trash, when he leaves your tennis racket outside in the rain or loses his bicycle—remember that these behaviors are typical of childhood. It is, more than likely, the mechanism by which an immature mind is protected from adult anxieties and pressures.

Be gentle as you teach him to do better. If he fails to respond to your patient instruction, it then becomes appropriate to administer some well-defined consequences. For example, he may have to work to pay for the item he abused or be deprived of its use. However, childish irresponsibility is very different from willful defiance, and should be handled more patiently.

4. *Reassure and teach after the confrontation is over.*

After a time of conflict during which the parent has demonstrated his right to lead (particularly if it resulted in tears for the child), the youngster between two and seven (or older) may want to be loved and reassured.

By all means, open your arms and let him come! Hold him close and tell him of your love. Rock him gently and let him know, again, why he was punished and how he can avoid the trouble next time. This moment of communication builds love, fidelity, and family unity.

And for the Christian family, it is extremely important to pray with the child at that time, admitting to God that we have *all* sinned and no one is perfect. Divine forgiveness is a marvelous experience, even for a very young child.

5. *Avoid impossible demands.*

Be absolutely sure that your child is *capable* of delivering what you require. Never punish him for wetting the bed involuntarily, or for not becoming potty-trained by one year of age, or for doing poorly in school when he is incapable of academic success. These impossible demands put the child in an unresolvable conflict: there is no way out. That condition brings inevitable damage to a human emotional apparatus.

6. *Let love be your guide!*

A relationship characterized by genuine love and affection is likely to be a healthy one, even though some parental mistakes and errors are inevitable.

SHOULD YOU SPANK YOUR CHILD?

With those six guidelines providing our background, let's turn our attention now to the more specific tools and techniques for shaping the will. We'll begin by discussing the practice of spanking, which has been the subject of heated controversy in recent years. More foolishness has been written on this subject than all other aspects of child rearing combined. Consider the views of Dr. John Valusek, a psychologist with whom I appeared on the Phil Donahue television show:

The way to stop violence in America is to stop spanking children, argues psychologist John Valusek. In a speech to the Utah Association for Mental Health some weeks ago, Valusek declared that parental spanking promotes the thesis that violence against others is acceptable.

"Spanking is the first half-inch on the yardstick of violence," said Valusek. "It is followed by hitting and ultimately by rape, murder, and assassination. The modeling behavior that occurs at home sets the stage: 'I will resort to violence when I don't know what else to do.'"[1]

To Dr. Valusek and his permissive colleagues I can only say, "Poppycock!" How ridiculous to blame America's obsession with violence on the disciplinary efforts of loving parents!

This conclusion is especially foolish in view of the bloody fare offered to our children on television each day. The average sixteen-year-old has watched 18,000 murders during his formative years, including a daily bombardment of knifings, shootings, hangings, decapitations, and general dismemberment.

Thus, it does seem strange that the psychological wizards of our day search elsewhere for the cause of brutality—and eventually point the finger of blame at the parents who are diligently training our future responsible citizens. Yet this is the kind of "press" that has been given in recent years to parents who believe in spanking their disobedient children.

FOUR FALLACIES ABOUT SPANKING

Opposition to corporal punishment can be summarized by four common arguments, all of them based on error and misunderstanding.

1. The first is represented by Dr. Valusek's statement and assumes that *spankings teach children to hit and hurt others*. It depicts corporal punishment as a hostile physical attack by an angry parent whose purpose is to damage or inflict harm on his little victim.

Admittedly, that kind of violence does occur regularly between generations and is tremendously destructive to children. (It is called child abuse and is discussed in Chapter 4.)

However, corporal punishment in the hands of a loving parent is altogether different in purpose and practice. It is a teaching tool by which harmful behavior is inhibited, rather than a wrathful attempt by one person to damage another. One is an act of love; the other is an act of hostility; and they are as different as night and day.

I responded to Dr. Valusek's argument in *Hide or Seek,* showing the place of minor pain in teaching children to behave responsibly:

> Those same specialists also say that a spanking teaches your child to hit others, making him a more violent person.
>
> Nonsense! If your child has ever bumped his arm against a hot stove, you can bet he'll never deliberately do that again. He does not become a more violent person because the stove burnt him. In fact, he learned a valuable lesson from the pain. Similarly, when he falls out of his high chair or smashes his finger in the door or is bitten by a grumpy dog, he learns about the physical dangers in his world.
>
> These bumps and bruises throughout childhood are nature's way of teaching him what to treat with respect. They do not damage his self-esteem. They do not make him vicious. They merely acquaint him with reality.
>
> In like manner, an appropriate spanking from a loving parent provides the same service. It tells him there are not only physical dangers to be

avoided, but he must steer clear of some social traps as well (selfishness, defiance, dishonesty, unprovoked aggression, etc.).[2]

2. The second rationale against corporal punishment can also be found in Dr. Valusek's concluding sentence, "I will resort to violence [spankings] when I don't know what else to do."

Do you see the subtlety of this quotation? It characterizes *a spanking as an absolute last resort—the final act of exasperation and frustration*. As such, it comes on the heels of screaming, threatening, hand-wringing, and buckets of tears. Even those authorities who recommend corporal punishment often fall into this trap, suggesting that it be applied only when all else has failed. I couldn't disagree more strongly.

A spanking is to be reserved for use in response to willful defiance, *whenever it occurs*. Period! It is much more effective to apply it early in the conflict, while the parent's emotional apparatus is still under control, than after ninety minutes of scratching and clawing.

In fact, child abuse is more likely to occur when a little youngster is permitted to irritate and agitate and sass and disobey and pout for hours, until finally the parent's anger reaches a point of explosion where anything can happen (and often does). Professionals like Dr. Valusek have inadvertently contributed to violence against children, in my view, because they have stripped parents of the right to correct children's routine behavior problems while they are of minor irritation. Then when these small frustrations accumulate, the parent does (as Valusek said) "resort to violence when [he doesn't] know what else to do."

3. The third common argument against spanking comes from the findings of animal psychology. If a mouse is running in a maze, he will learn much faster if the experimenter rewards his correct turns with food than he will if his incorrect choices are punished with a mild electric shock. From this and similar studies has come the incredible assumption that *punishment has little influence on human behavior.* But human beings are not mice, and it is naive to equate them simplistically.

Obviously, a child is capable of rebellious and defiant attitudes that have no relevance to a puzzled mouse sitting at a crossroads in a maze. I agree that it would not help a boy or girl learn to read by shocking him or her for each mispronounced word. On the other hand, deliberate disobedience involves the child's perception of parental authority and his obligations to accept it (whereas the mouse does not even know the experimenter exists).

If punishment doesn't influence human behavior, then why is the issuance of speeding citations by police so effective in controlling traffic on a busy street? Why, then, do homeowners rush to get their tax payments in the mail to avoid a 6 percent penalty for being late? If punishment has no power, then why does a well-deserved spanking often turn a sullen little troublemaker into a sweet and loving angel?

Rat psychology notwithstanding, both reward and punishment play an important role in shaping human behavior, and neither should be discounted.

> "He who does not punish evil commands it to be done!"
>
> —Leonardo da Vinci

4. The fourth argument against the judicious practice of spanking says that *it damages the dignity and self-worth of the child.*

This subject is so important that I have devoted an entire chapter to preserving the spirit (see Chapter 4). Suffice it to say at this point that a child is fully capable of discerning whether his parent is conveying love or hatred. This is why the youngster who knows he deserves a spanking appears almost relieved when it finally comes. Rather than being insulted by the discipline, he understands its purpose and appreciates the control it gives him over his own impulses.

This childish comprehension was beautifully illustrated by a father who told me of a time when his five-year-old son was disobeying in a restaurant. This lad was sassing his mother, flipping water on his younger brother, and deliberately making a nuisance of himself. After four warnings which went unheeded, the father took his son by the arm and marched him to the parking lot where he proceeded to administer a spanking.

Watching this episode was a meddling woman who had followed them out of the restaurant and into the parking lot. When the punishment began, she shook her finger at the father and screamed, "Leave that boy alone! Turn him loose! If you don't stop I'm going to call the police!"

The five-year-old, who had been crying and jumping, immediately stopped yelling and said to his father in surprise, "What's wrong with that woman, Dad?" He understood the purpose for the discipline, even if the "rescuer" didn't. I only wish that Dr. Valusek and his contemporaries were as perceptive as this child.

CHAPTER
3

Steps to Discipline for Every Age

Let me hasten to emphasize that corporal punishment is not the only tool for use in shaping the will, nor is it appropriate at all ages and for all situations. The wise parent must understand the physical and emotional characteristics of each stage in childhood, and then fit the discipline to a boy's or girl's individual needs.

Perhaps I can assist in that process now by listing specific age categories and offering a few practical suggestions and examples for the various time frames. Please understand that this discussion is by no means exhaustive, and merely suggests the general nature of disciplinary methods at specific periods.

> **Wise parents fit the discipline to a boy's or girl's individual needs.**

BIRTH TO SEVEN MONTHS

No *direct* discipline is necessary for a child under seven months of age, regardless of behavior or circumstance. Many parents do not agree, and find themselves "swatting" a child of six months for wiggling while being diapered or for crying in the midnight hours. This is a serious mistake.

A baby is incapable of comprehending his "offense" or associating it with the resulting punishment. At this early age, he needs to be held, loved, and most important, hear a soothing human voice. He should be fed when hungry and kept clean and dry and warm. In essence, it is probable that the foundation for emotional and physical health is laid during this first six-month period, which should be characterized by security, affection, and warmth.

On the other hand, it is possible to create a fussy, demanding baby by rushing to pick him up every time he utters a whimper or sigh. Infants are fully capable of learning to manipulate their parents through a process called reinforcement, whereby any behavior that produces a pleasant result will tend to recur. Thus, a healthy baby can keep his mother hopping around his nursery twelve hours a day (or night) by simply forcing air past his sandpaper larynx.

To avoid this consequence, it is important to strike a balance between giving your baby the attention he needs and establishing him as a tiny dictator. Don't be afraid to let him cry a reasonable period of time (which is thought to be healthy for the lungs) although it is necessary

Do You Have a Difficult Baby?

Yes, Virginia, there *are* easy babies and there are difficult babies! Some seem determined to dismantle the homes into which they were born; they sleep cozily during the day and then howl in protest all night; they get colic and spit up the vilest stuff on their clothes (usually on the way to church); they control their internal plumbing until you hand them to strangers, and then let it blast. Instead of cuddling into the fold of the arms when being held, they stiffen rigidly in search of freedom. And to be honest, a mother may find herself leaning cockeyed over a vibrating crib at 3:00 a.m., asking the eternal question, "What's it all about, Alfie?"* A few days earlier she was wondering, "Will he survive?" Now she is asking, "Will *I* survive?!"

But believe it or not, both generations will probably recover and this disruptive beginning will be nothing but a dim memory for the parents in such a brief moment. And from that demanding tyrant will grow a thinking, loving human being with an eternal soul and a special place in the heart of the Creator. To the exhausted and harassed new mother, let me say, "Hang tough! You are doing *the* most important job in the universe!"

---

*Someone has suggested that babies be fed a combination of oatmeal and garlic for dinner each evening. The stuff tastes terrible, of course, but it does help parents locate their kids in the dark! (Please don't take this suggestion literally.)

to listen to the tone of his voice for the difference between random discontent and genuine distress. Most mothers learn to recognize this distinction in time.

EIGHT TO FOURTEEN MONTHS

Many children will begin to test the authority of their parents during the second seven-month period. The confrontations will be minor and infrequent before the first birthday, yet the beginnings of future struggles can be seen.

My own daughter, for example, challenged her mother for the first time when she was nine months old. My wife was waxing the kitchen floor when Danae crawled to the edge of the linoleum. Shirley said, "No, Danae," gesturing to the child not to enter the kitchen.

Since our daughter began talking very early, she clearly understood the meaning of the word *no*. Nevertheless, she crawled straight onto the sticky wax. Shirley picked her up and sat her down in the doorway, while saying, "No," more firmly.

Not to be discouraged, Danae scrambled onto the newly mopped floor. My wife took her back, saying, "No" even more strongly as she put her down.

Seven times this process was repeated, until Danae finally yielded and crawled away in tears. As far as we can recall, that was the first direct collision of wills between my daughter and wife. Many more were to follow. How does a parent discipline a one-year-old? Very carefully and gently! A child at this age is extremely easy to distract and divert. Rather than jerking a china cup from his hands, show him a brightly colored alternative—and then be prepared to catch the cup when it falls.

When unavoidable confrontations do occur, as with Danae on the waxy floor, win them by firm persistence but not by punishment. Again, don't be afraid of the child's tears, which can become a potent weapon to avoid naptime or bedtime or diapertime. *Have the courage to lead the child without being harsh or mean or gruff.*

Compared to the months that are to follow, the period around one year of age is usually a tranquil, smooth-functioning time in a child's life.

FIFTEEN TO TWENTY-FOUR MONTHS

It has been said that all human beings can be classified into two broad categories: those who would vote "yes" to the various propositions of life, and those who would vote "no."

I can tell you with confidence that each toddler around the world would definitely cast a negative vote! If there is one word that characterizes the period between fifteen and twenty-four months of age, it is *No!* No, he doesn't want to eat his cereal. No, he doesn't want to play with his dump truck. No, he doesn't want to take his bath. And you can be sure, no, he doesn't want to go to bed anytime at all. It is easy to see why this period of life has been called "the first adolescence," because of the negativism, conflict, and defiance that characterize it.

Dr. T. Berry Brazelton has written a beautiful description of the "terrible twos" in his excellent book *Toddlers and Parents*. (I enthusiastically recommend this book to anyone wanting to understand this fascinating and challenging age.) Quoted below is a classic depiction of a typical eighteen-month-old boy named Greg.[1] Although I have never met the fellow, I know him well . . . as you will when your child becomes a toddler.

When Greg began to be negative in the second year, his parents felt as if they had been hit with a sledgehammer. His good nature seemed submerged under a load of negatives. When his parents asked anything of him, his mouth took on a grim set, his eyes narrowed, and, facing them squarely with his penetrating look, he replied simply "no!" When offered ice cream, which he loved, he preceded his acceptance with a "no." While he rushed to get his snowsuit to go outside, he said "no" to going out.

His parents' habit of watching Greg for cues now began to turn sour. He seemed to be fighting with them all of the time. When he was asked to perform a familiar chore, his response was, "I can't." When his mother tried to stop him from emptying his clothes drawer, his response was, "I have to." He pushed hard on every familiar imposed limit, and never seemed satisfied until his parent collapsed in defeat.

He would turn on the television set when his mother left the room. When she returned, she turned it off, scolded Greg mildly, and left again. He turned it on. She came rushing back to reason with him, to ask him why he'd disobeyed her. He replied, "I have to." The intensity of her insistence that he leave it alone increased. He looked steadily back at her. She returned to the kitchen. He turned it on. She was waiting behind the door, swirled in to slap his hands firmly. He sighed deeply and said, "I have to." She sat down beside him, begging him to listen to her to avoid real punishment. Again he presented a dour mask with knitted brows to her, listening but not listening. She rose wearily, walked out again. Just as wearily, he walked over to the machine to turn it on. As she came right back, tears in her eyes, to spank him, she said, "Greg, why do you want me to spank you? I hate it!" To which he replied, "I have to." As she crumpled in her chair, weeping softly with him across her lap, Greg reached up to touch her wet face.

After this clash, Mrs. Lang was exhausted. Greg sensed this and began to try to be helpful. He ran to the kitchen to fetch her mop and her dustpan, which he dragged in to her as she sat in her chair. This reversal made her smile and she gathered him up in a hug.

Greg caught her change in mood and danced off gaily to a corner, where he slid behind a chair, saying "hi and see." As he pushed the chair out, he tipped over a lamp which went crashing to the floor. His mother's reaction was a loud "No, Greg!" He curled up on the floor, his hands over his ears, eyes tightly closed, as if he were trying to shut out all the havoc he had wrought.

As soon as he was put into his high chair, he began to whine. She was so surprised that she stopped preparation of his food, and took him to change him. This did not settle the issue, and when she brought him to his chair again, he began to squirm and twist. She let him down to play until his lunch was ready. He lay on the floor, alternately whining and screeching. So unusual was this that she felt his diaper for pins which might be unclasped, felt his forehead for fever and wondered whether to give him an aspirin. Finally, she returned to fixing his lunch. Without an audience Greg subsided.

When she placed him in his chair again, his shrill whines began anew. She placed his plate in front of him with cubes of food to spear with his fork. He tossed the implement overboard, and began to push his plate away, refusing the food. Mrs. Lang was nonplussed, decided he didn't feel well, and offered him his favorite ice cream. Again, he sat helpless, refusing to feed himself. When she offered him some of the mush, he submissively allowed himself to be fed a few spoonfuls. Then he knocked the spoon out of her hand and pushed the ice cream away. Mrs. Lang was sure he was ill.

Mrs. Lang extracted Greg from his embattled position, and placed him on the floor to play while she ate her own lunch. This, of course, wasn't what he wanted either. He continued to tease her, asking for food off her plate, which he devoured greedily. His eagerness disproved her theory of illness. When she ignored him and continued to eat, his efforts redoubled. He climbed under the sink to find the bleach bottle which he brought to her on command. He fell forward onto the floor and cried loudly as if he'd hurt himself. He began to grunt as if he were having a bowel movement and to pull on his pants. This was almost a sure way of dragging his mother away from her own activity, for she'd started trying to "catch" him and put him on the toilet. This was one of his signals for her attention, and she rushed him to the toilet. He smiled smugly at her, but refused to perform. Mrs. Lang felt as if she were suddenly embattled on all fronts—none of which she could win.

When she turned to her own chores, Greg produced the bowel movement he'd been predicting.

The picture sounds pretty bleak, and admittedly, there are times when a little toddler can dismantle the peace and tranquillity of a home. (My son Ryan loved to blow bubbles in the dog's water dish—a game which still horrifies me.)

However, with all of its struggles, *there is no more thrilling time of life* than this period of dynamic blossoming and unfolding. New words are being learned daily, and the cute verbal expressions of that age will be remembered for a half century. It is a time of excitement over fairy stories and Santa Claus and furry puppy dogs. And most important, it is a precious time of loving and warmth that will scurry by all too quickly. There are millions of older parents today with grown children who would give all they possess to relive those bubbly days with their toddlers.

TIPS FOR SURVIVING THE TERRIBLE TWOS

Let me make a few disciplinary recommendations which will, I hope, ease some of the tension of the toddler experience. I must hasten to say, however, that the negativism of this turbulent period is both normal and healthy, and *nothing* will make an eighteen-month-old child act like a five-year-old.

1. First, and for obvious reasons, *it is extremely important for fathers to help discipline and participate in the parenting process when possible.*

Children need their fathers and respond to their masculine manner, of course, but wives need their husbands, too. This is especially true of housewives, such as Greg's mother, who have done combat duty through the long day and find themselves in a state of battle fatigue by nightfall. Husbands get tired too, of course, but if they can hold together long enough to help get the little tigers in bed, nothing could contribute more to the stability of their homes!

I am especially sympathetic with the mother who is raising her toddler of two and an infant at the same time. There is no more difficult assignment on the face of the earth. Husbands who recognize this fact can help their wives feel understood, loved, and supported in the vital jobs they are doing.

2. *For the strong-willed toddler, mild spankings can begin between fifteen and eighteen months of age.* They should be relatively infrequent, and must be reserved for the kind of defiance Greg displayed over the television set. He clearly knew what his mother wanted, but refused to comply. He should *not* have been spanked for knocking over the lamp or for the bowel movement episode or for refusing to eat his ice cream. A heavy hand of authority during this period causes the child to suppress his need to experiment and test

his environment, which can have long-lasting consequences.

To repeat, the toddler should be taught to obey and yield to parental leadership, but that end result will not be accomplished overnight.

3. *Administer spankings with a neutral object— that is, a small switch or belt—but rarely with the hand!*

I have always felt that the hand should be seen by the child as an object of love rather than an instrument of punishment. Furthermore, if a parent commonly slaps a youngster when he is not expecting to be hit, then he will probably duck and flinch whenever Father suddenly scratches his ear. And, of course, a slap in the face can reposition the nose or do permanent damage to the ears or jaw.

If all spankings are administered with a neutral object, applied where intended, then the child need never fear that he will suddenly be chastised for some accidental indiscretion. (There are exceptions to this rule, such as when a child's hands are slapped or thumped for reaching for a stove or other dangerous object.)

4. *A spanking should hurt or else it will have no influence.* A swat on the behind through three layers of wet diapers simply conveys no urgent message. However, a small amount of pain for a young child goes a long way; it is certainly not necessary to lash or "whip" him. Two or three stinging strokes on the legs or bottom with a switch are usually sufficient to emphasize the point, "You must obey me."

5. *Spank immediately after the offense, or not at all.* A toddler's memory is not sufficiently developed to permit even a ten-minute delay in the administration of justice.

6. *After the episode is over and the tears have subsided, hold and reassure your child.* Embrace him in the security of your loving arms. Rock him softly. Tell him how much you love him and why he must "mind his mommy." This moment can be the most important event in the entire day.

7. *Do not punish toddlers for behavior that is natural and necessary to learning and development.* Exploration of their environment, for example, is of great importance to intellectual stimulation.

You and I as adults will look at a crystal trinket and obtain whatever information we seek from that visual inspection. A toddler, however, will expose it to all of his senses. He will pick it up, taste it, smell it, wave it in the air, pound it on the wall, throw it across the room, and listen to the pretty sound that it makes when shattering. By that process he learns a bit about gravity, rough versus smooth surfaces, the brittle nature of glass, and some startling things about mother's anger.

Am I suggesting that children be allowed to destroy a home and all of its contents? No, but neither is it right to expect a curious child to keep his hands to himself. Parents should remove those items that are fragile or particularly dangerous, and then strew the child's path with fascinating objects of all types. Permit him to explore everything possible and do not ever punish him for touching something that he *did not know was off limits,* regardless of its value.

With respect to dangerous items, such as electric plugs and stoves, as well as a few untouchable objects, such as the knobs on the television set, it is possible and necessary to teach and enforce the command, "Don't touch!" After making it clear what is expected, a thump on the fingers or slap on the hands will usually discourage repeat episodes.

Entire books have been written on the subject which I have only touched here. Nevertheless, I hope this brief introduction will give the "flavor" of discipline for the young toddler.

TWO TO THREE YEARS

Perhaps the most frustrating aspect of the "terrible twos" is the tendency of kids to spill things, destroy things, eat horrible things, fall off things, flush things, kill things, and get into things. They also have a knack for doing embarrassing things, like sneezing on a nearby man at a lunch counter.

During these toddler years, any unexplained silence of more than thirty seconds can throw an adult into a sudden state of panic. What mother has not had the thrill of opening the bedroom door, only to find Tony Tornado covered with lipstick from the top of his pink head to the carpet on which he stands? On the wall is his own artistic creation with a red handprint in the center, and throughout the room is the aroma of Chanel No. 5 with which he has anointed his

Test Findings: What Makes a Happy, Healthy Child

I would like to share with you the results of an extremely important ten-year study of children between eight and eighteen months of age. This investigation, known as Harvard University's Preschool Project, was guided by Dr. Burton L. White and a team of fifteen researchers between 1965 and 1975. They studied young children intensely during this period, hoping to discover which experiences in the early years of life contribute to the development of a healthy, intelligent human being. The conclusions from this exhaustive effort are summarized below, as reported originally in the *APA Monitor*.[2]

1. It is increasingly clear that the origins of human competence are to be found in *a critical period of development* between eight and eighteen months of age. The child's experiences during these brief months do more to influence future intellectual competence than any time before or after.
2. The single most important environmental factor in the life of the child is *his mother*. "She is on the hook," said Dr. White, and carries more influence on her child's experiences than any other person or circumstance.
3. The amount of *live language* directed to a child (not to be confused with television, radio, or overheard conversations) is vital to his development of fundamental

linguistic, intellectual, and social skills. The researchers concluded, "Providing a rich social life for a twelve- to fifteen-month-old child is the best thing you can do to guarantee a good mind."

4. Those children who are given *free access* to living areas of their homes progressed much faster than those whose movements are restricted.

5. The *nuclear family* is the most important educational delivery system. If we are going to produce capable, healthy children, it will be by strengthening family units and by improving the interactions that occur within them.

6. The best parents were those who excelled at *three key functions*:

   • They were superb designers and organizers of their children's environments.
   • They permitted their children to interrupt them for brief thirty-second episodes, during which personal consultation, comfort, information, and enthusiasm were exchanged.
   • THEY WERE FIRM DISCIPLINARIANS WHILE SIMULTANEOUSLY SHOWING GREAT AFFECTION FOR THEIR CHILDREN. (My emphasis added. I couldn't have said it better myself.)

   Do these results speak dramatically to anyone but me? I hear within them an affirmation and validation of the concepts to which I have devoted my professional life.

baby brother. Wouldn't it be interesting to hold a national convention sometime, bringing together all the mothers who have experienced that exact trauma?

When my daughter was two years of age, she was fascinated the first time she watched me shave in the morning. She stood captivated as I soaped my face and began using the razor. That should have been my first clue that something was up. The following morning, Shirley came into the bathroom to find our dachshund, Siggie, sitting in his favorite spot on the furry lid of the toilet seat. Danae had covered his head with lather and was systematically shaving the hair from his shiny skull! Shirley screamed, "Danae!" which sent Siggie and his barber scurrying for safety. It was a strange sight to see the frightened dog with nothing but ears sticking up on the top of his bald head.

When Ryan was the same age, he had an incredible ability to make messes. He could turn it over or spill it faster than any kid I've ever seen, especially at mealtime. (Once while eating a peanut butter sandwich he thrust his hand through the bottom side. When his fingers emerged at the top they were covered with peanut butter, and Ryan didn't recognize them. The poor lad nearly bit off his index finger.)

Because of his destructive inclination, Ryan heard the word "mess" used repeatedly by his parents. It became one of the most important words in his vocabulary. One evening while taking a shower I left the door ajar and got some water on the floor. And as you might expect, Ryan came thumping around the corner and stepped in it. He looked up at me and said in the gruffest voice he could manage, "Whuss all this mess in hyere?"

HOW TO HANDLE THE OLDER TODDLER

You *must* keep a sense of humor during the twos and threes in order to preserve your own sanity. But you must also proceed with the task of instilling obedience and respect for authority. Thus, most of the comments written in the preceding section also apply to the child between twenty-two and thirty-six months of age.

Although the "older" toddler is much different physically and emotionally than he was at eighteen months, the tendency to test and challenge parental authority is still very much in evidence. In fact, when the young toddler consistently wins the early confrontations and conflicts, he becomes even more difficult to handle in the second and third years. Then a lifelong disrespect for authority often begins to settle into his young mind.

Therefore, I cannot overemphasize the importance of instilling two distinct messages within your child before he is forty-eight months of age: (1) "I love you more than you can possibly understand. You are precious to me and I thank God every day that He let me raise you!" (2) "Because I love you, I must teach you to obey me. That is the only way I can take care of you and protect you from things that might hurt you. Let's read what the Bible tells us: 'Children, obey your parents; this is the right thing to do because God has placed them in authority over you'" (Eph. 6:1).

Healthy parenthood can be boiled down to those two essential ingredients, love and control, operating in a system of checks and balances. Any concentration on love to the exclusion of control usually breeds disrespect and contempt. Conversely, an authoritarian and oppressive home atmosphere is deeply resented by the child who feels unloved or even hated. To repeat, the objective for the toddler years is to strike a balance between mercy and justice, affection and authority, love and control.

> **Healthy parenthood can be boiled down to those two essential ingredients, love and control, operating in a system of checks and balances.**

DISCIPLINE THAT MAKES SENSE

Specifically, how does one discipline a "naughty" two- or three-year-old child? One possible approach is to require the boy or girl to sit in a chair and think about what he has done. Most children of this age are bursting with energy, and absolutely hate to spend ten dull minutes with their wiggly posteriors glued to a chair. To some individuals, this form of punishment can be even more effective than a spanking, and is remembered longer.

Parents to whom I have made that recommendation have often said, "But what if he won't stay in the chair?" The same questions is asked with reference to the child's tendency to pop out of bed after being tucked in at night. These are examples of the direct confrontations I have been describing. The parent who cannot require a toddler to stay on a chair or in his bed is not yet in command of the child. There is no better time than now to change the relationship.

I would suggest the following procedure.

1. Place the youngster in bed and give him a little speech, such as "Johnny, this time Mommy means business. Are you listening to me? *Do not* get out of this bed. Do you understand me?"

2. When Johnny's feet touch the floor, give him one swat on the legs with a small switch. Put the switch on his dresser where he can see it, and promise him one more stroke if he gets up again. Walk confidently out of the room without further comment.

3. If Johnny rebounds again, fulfill your promise and offer the same warning if he doesn't stay in bed.

4. Repeat the episode until Johnny acknowledges that you are the boss. Then hug him, tell him you love him, and remind him how important it is for him to get his rest so that he won't be sick, etc.

Your purpose in this painful exercise (painful for both parties) is not only to keep li'l John in bed, but to confirm your leadership in his mind. It is my opinion that too many American parents lack the courage to win this kind of confrontation, and are off-balance and defensive ever after. Dr. Benjamin Spock wrote in 1974, "Inability to be firm is, to my mind, the commonest problem of parents in America today." I agree.

FOUR TO EIGHT YEARS

By the time a child reaches four years of age, the focus of discipline should be not only on his behavior, but also on the *attitudes* which motivate it. This task of shaping the personality can be relatively simple or incredibly difficult, depending on the basic temperament of a particular child.

Some youngsters are naturally warm and loving and trusting, while others sincerely believe the world is out to get them. Some enjoy giving and sharing, whereas their siblings are consistently selfish and demanding. Some smile throughout the day while others complain and bellyache about everything from toothpaste to turnip greens.

Furthermore, these attitudinal patterns are not consistent from one time to the next. They tend to alternate cyclically between rebellion and obedience. In other words, a time of intense conflict and defiance (if properly handled) gives way to a period of love and cooperation. Then when Mom and Dad relax and congratulate themselves for doing a super job of parenting, their little chameleon changes colors again.

Some might ask, "So what? Why should we be concerned about the attitudes of a boy or girl?" Indeed, there are many child-rearing specialists who suggest that parents ignore negative attitudes, including those which are unmistakably defiant in tone. Consider the naive recommendations of Dr. Luther Woodward, as paraphrased in the book for parents, *Your Child from Two to Five*.

> What do you do when your preschooler calls you a "big stinker" or threatens to flush you down the toilet? Do you scold, punish . . . or sensibly take it in your stride? . . .
>
> Dr. Woodward recommends a positive policy of understanding as the best and fastest way to help a child outgrow this verbal violence. When parents fully realize that all little tots feel angry and destructive at times, they are better able to minimize these outbursts. Once the preschooler gets rid of his hostility, the desire to destroy is gone and instinctive feelings of love and affection have a chance to sprout and grow. Once the child is six or seven, parents can rightly let the child know that he is expected to be outgrowing sassing his parents.

In conclusion, Dr. Woodward reveals the permissive implications of his recommendation by warning those who try to apply it:

> But this policy takes a broad perspective and a lot of composure, especially when friends and relatives voice disapproval and warn you that you are bringing up a brat.[3]

In this case, your friends and relatives will probably be right. This suggestion (published during the permissive 1950s and so typical of other writings from that era) is based on the simplistic notion that children will develop sweet and loving attitudes if we adults will permit and encourage their temper tantrums during childhood. According to the optimistic Dr. Woodward, the tot who has been calling his mother a "big stinker" for six or seven years can be expected to embrace her suddenly in love and dignity.

That outcome is most improbable. Dr. Woodward's creative "policy of understanding" (which means, stand and do nothing) offers a one-way ticket to emotional and social disaster, in my view.

I expressed my contrasting opinion in my book *The New Dare to Discipline*:

> If it is desirable that children be kind, appreciative, and pleasant, those qualities should be taught—not hoped for. If we want to see honesty, truthfulness, and unselfishness in our offspring, then these characteristics should be the conscious objectives of our early instructional process. If it is important to produce respectful, responsible young citizens, then we should set out to mold them accordingly. The point is obvious: *heredity does not equip a child with proper attitudes; children will learn what they are taught.* We cannot expect the desirable attitudes and behavior to appear if we have not done our early homework.[4]

TWO WAYS TO SHAPE ATTITUDES

But *how* does one shape the attitudes of children? Most parents find it easier to deal with outright disobedience than with unpleasant characteristics of temperament or personality. Let me restate two age-old suggestions for parents, and then I'll offer a system which can be used with the especially disagreeable child.

1. *There is no substitute for parental modeling of the attitudes we wish to teach.* Someone wrote, "The footsteps a child follows are most likely to be the ones his parents thought they covered up." It is true. Our children are watching us carefully, and they instinctively imitate our behavior.

- We can hardly expect them to be kind and giving if we are consistently grouchy and selfish.
- We will be unable to teach appreciativeness if we never say "please" or "thank you" at home or abroad.
- We will not produce honest children if we teach them to lie to the bill collector on the phone by saying, "Dad's not home."

In these matters, our boys and girls instantly discern the gap between what we say and what we do. And of the two choices, they usually identify with our behavior and ignore our empty proclamations.

2. *Most of the favorable attitudes which should be taught are actually extrapolations of the Judeo-Christian ethic.* These include honesty, respect, kindness, love, human dignity, obedience, responsibility, and reverence.

And how are these time-honored principles conveyed to the next generation? The answer was provided by Moses as he wrote more than

4,000 years ago in the book of Deuteronomy. "You must teach them to your children and talk about them when you are at home or out for a walk; at bedtime and the first thing in the morning. Tie them on your finger, wear them on your forehead, and write them on the doorposts of your house" (Deut. 6:7-9).

In other words, we can't instill these attitudes during a brief, two-minute bedtime prayer, or during formalized training sessions. We must *live* them from morning to night. They should be reinforced during our casual conversation, punctuated with illustrations, and emphasized through demonstrations, compliments, and chastisement. This teaching task is, I believe, *the* most important assignment God has given to us as parents.

> **Our boys and girls instantly discern the gap between what we say and what we do.**

THE ATTITUDE CHART

Finally, let me suggest an approach for use with the strong-willed or negative child (age six or older) for whom other forms of instruction have been ineffective. I am referring specifically to the sour, complaining child who is making himself and the rest of the family miserable. He may slide his brakes for weeks and criticize the efforts of everyone nearby.

The problem with such an individual is in defining the changes that are desired and then reinforcing the improvements when they occur. Attitudes are abstractions that a six- or eight-year-old may not fully understand, and we need a system that will clarify the "target" in his mind.

Toward this end, I have developed an Attitude Chart (see illustration) which translates these

MY ATTITUDE CHART FOR _____

	1 Excellent	2 Good	3 Okay	4 Bad	5 Terrible
My Attitude toward Mom					
My Attitude toward Dad					
My Attitude toward Sister/Brother					
My Attitude toward Friends					
My Attitude toward Work					
My Attitude at Bedtime					

DATE

TOTAL POINTS _____

CONSEQUENCES
6-9 points	The family will do something fun together
10-18 points	Nothing happens, good or bad
19-20 points	I have to stay in my room for one hour
21-22 points	I get one swat with paddle
23+ points	I get two swats with paddle

subtle mannerisms into concrete mathematical terms. *Please note:* This system would *not* be appropriate for the child who merely has a bad day, or displays temporary unpleasantness associated with illness, fatigue, or environmental circumstances. Rather, it is a *remedial tool* to help change persistently negative and disrespectful attitudes by making the child conscious of his problem.

The Attitude Chart should be prepared and then reproduced, since a separate sheet will be needed every day. Place an X in the appropriate square for each category, and then add the total points "earned" by bedtime.

Although this nightly evaluation process has the appearance of being objective to a child, it is obvious that the parent can influence the outcome (it's called cheating). Mom or Dad may want Junior to receive eighteen points on the first night, barely missing the punishment but realizing he must stretch the following day.

I must emphasize that the system will fail miserably if a naughty child does not receive the punishment he deserves, or if he hustles to improve but does not obtain the family fun he was promised. This approach is nothing more than a method of applying reward and punishment to attitudes in a way that children can understand and remember.

For the child who does not fully comprehend the concept of numbers, it might be helpful to plot the daily totals on a cumulative graph, such as the one illustrated.

I don't expect everyone to appreciate this

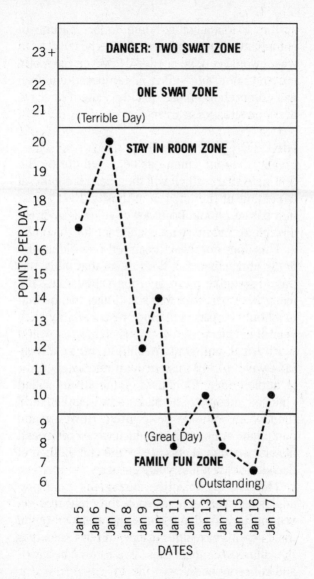

system or to apply it at home. In fact, parents of compliant, happy children will be puzzled as to why it would ever be needed. However, the mothers and fathers of sullen, ill-tempered children will comprehend more quickly. Take it or leave it, as the situation warrants.

NINE TO TWELVE YEARS

Ideally, the foundation has been laid during the first nine years which will then permit a general loosening of the lines of authority. Every year that passes should bring fewer rules, less direct discipline, and more independence for the child.

This does not mean that a ten-year-old is suddenly emancipated; it does mean that he is permitted to make more decisions about his daily living than when he was six. It also means that he should be carrying more responsibility each year of his life.

Physical punishment should be relatively *infrequent* during this period immediately prior to adolescence. Of course, some strong-willed children absolutely demand to be spanked, and their wishes should be granted. However, the compliant youngster should have experienced his last woodshed episode by the end of his first decade (or even four years earlier).

The overall objective during the final pre-adolescent period is to teach the child that his actions have inevitable consequences. One of the most serious casualties in a permissive society is the failure to connect those two factors, behavior and consequences.

- A three-year-old child screams insults at his mother, but Mom stands blinking her eyes in confusion.
- A first-grader launches an attack on his teacher, but the school makes allowances for his age and takes no action.
- A ten-year-old is caught stealing candy in a store, but is released to the recognizance of his parents.
- A fifteen-year-old sneaks the keys to the family car, but his father pays the fine when he is arrested.
- A seventeen-year-old drives his Chevy like a maniac and his parents pay for the repairs when he wraps it around a telephone pole.

You see, all through childhood, loving parents seem determined to intervene between behavior and consequences, breaking the connection and preventing the valuable learning that could have occurred.

Thus, it is possible for a young man or woman to enter adult life, not really knowing that life bites—that every move we make directly affects our future—that irresponsible behavior eventually produces sorrow and pain. Such a person applies for his first job and arrives late for work three times during the first week; then, when he is fired in a flurry of hot words, he becomes bitter and frustrated. It was the first time in his life that Mom and Dad couldn't come running to rescue him from the unpleasant consequences.

(Unfortunately, many American parents still try to "bail out" their grown children even when they are in their twenties and live away from home.)

What is the result? This overprotection produces emotional cripples who often develop lasting characteristics of dependency and a kind of perpetual adolescence.

How does one connect behavior with conse-

An Ounce of Prevention Still Works

I was accompanied on a recent speaking trip by my wife, Shirley, which required us to leave our two children with their grandparents for a full week. My wife's mother and father are wonderful people and dearly love Danae and Ryan. However, two bounding, jumping, giggling little rascals can wear down the nerves of *any* adult, especially those who are approaching the age of retirement.

When we returned home from the trip I asked my father-in-law how the children behaved and whether or not they caused him any problems. He replied in his North Dakota (Lawrence Welk) accent, "Oh, no! Dere good kids. But the important thing is, you jus' got to keep 'em out in da open."

That was probably the best disciplinary advice ever offered. Many behavioral problems can be prevented by simply avoiding the circumstances that create them. And especially for boys and girls growing up in our congested cities, perhaps what we need most is to "get 'em out in da open." It's not a bad idea.

---

quences? By being willing to let the child experience a reasonable amount of pain when he behaves irresponsibly. When Jack misses the school bus through his own dawdling, let him walk a mile or two and enter school in midmorning (unless safety factors prevent this). If Janie carelessly loses her lunch money, let her skip a meal.

Obviously, it is possible to carry this principle too far, being harsh and inflexible with an immature child. But the best approach is to expect boys and girls to *carry the responsibility that is appropriate for their age*, and occasionally to taste the bitter fruit that irresponsibility bears.

There is so much that should be said about this late childhood era, but time and space limitations force me to move on. In conclusion, the period between ten and eleven years of age often represents a final time of great closeness and unpretentious love between parent and child. Enjoy it to the maximum, for believe me, there are more tumultuous days coming!

Your Child's Fragile Spirit

There are dangers implicit in what I have stated about discipline of the strong-willed child. The reader could assume that I perceive children as the villains and parents as the inevitable good guys. Of greater concern is the inference that I'm recommending a rigid, harsh, oppressive approach to discipline in the home. Neither statement is even partially accurate.

In contrast, I see small children (even those who challenge authority) as vulnerable little creatures who need buckets of love and tenderness every day of their lives. One of my great frustrations in teaching parents has been the difficulty in conveying a *balanced* environment, wherein discipline is evident when necessary, but where it is matched by patience and respect and affection. Let it never be said that I favor the "slap 'em across the mouth" approach to authoritarianism. That hostile manner not only wounds the spirit, but it's hard on teeth, too.

CHILD ABUSE AND ITS VICTIMS

No subject distresses me more than the phenomenon of child abuse which is so prevalent in America today. There are children all across this country, even while I write, who are suffering untold miseries at the hands of their parents. Some of these pitiful little tots are brought to our hospital in every imaginable condition. They have been burned and bruised and broken and their little minds are permanently warped by the awful circumstances into which they were born.

Every professional who works with hurt children has to learn to cope with his own empathy. I have gained a measure of control over my own emotions; however, I have never been able to observe a battered child without feeling a literal agony within my chest.

Diseased children suffer, of course, but most of them experience some measure of parental love which provides an emotional undergirding. But battered children suffer physically *and* emotionally. For them, no one cares. No one understands. There is no one to whom the longings can be expressed. They cannot escape. They cannot explain why they are hated. And many of them are too young to develop defense mechanisms or even call for help.

I dealt this spring with an eight-year-old girl who had been sexually assaulted repeatedly by her alcoholic father since she was fifteen months of age. What an immeasurable tragedy. Another child in Los Angeles was blinded by his mother, who destroyed his eyes with a razor blade. Can you imagine going through life knowing that your handicap resulted from a deliberate act by your own mother? Another small child in our city was pushed from a car on a crowded freeway and left clinging to the chain link divider for eight or nine hours. Another child's feet were held to a hot iron as punishment.

Recently, a radio news summary broadcast through my office intercom told of finding a ten-year-old girl hanging by her heels in her parents' garage. These kinds of horror stories are all too familiar to those of us who work with children. In fact, it is highly probable that some youngster within a mile or two of your house is experiencing destructive abuse in one manner or another.

> "Child abuse . . . once thought to be primarily a problem of the poor and downtrodden . . . occurs in every segment of society and may be the country's leading cause of death in children."
>
> —Brian G. Fraser, attorney for the National Center for Prevention and Treatment of Child Abuse and Neglect.

AVOIDING THE DOUBLE WHAMMY

The last thing on earth that I want to do is to provide a rationalization and justification for such parental oppression. Let me say it again: I don't believe in harsh, inflexible discipline, even when it is well intentioned. Children must be given room to breathe and grow and love. But there are also threatening circumstances at the permissive end of the spectrum, and many parents fall into one trap in an earnest attempt to avoid the other.

These dual dangers were beautifully described by Marguerite and Willard Beecher, writing in their book *Parents on the Run:*

> The adult-centered home of yesteryear made parents the masters and children their slaves. The child-centered home of today has made parents the slaves and children the masters. There is no true cooperation in any master-slave relationship, and therefore no democracy. Neither the restrictive-authoritative technique of rearing children nor the newer "anything-goes" technique develop the genius within the individual, because neither trains him to be self-reliant. . . .
>
> Children reared under arbitrary rules become either spineless automatons or bitter revolutionaries who waste their lives in conflict with those around them. But children who know no law higher than their own passing fancy become trapped by their own appetites. In either case, they are slaves. The former are enslaved by leaders on whom they depend to tell them what to do, and the latter are enslaved by the pawnbroker. Neither are (sic) capable of maintaining society on any decent basis. A lifetime of unhappiness may be avoided if the twig is bent so the tree will not incline in either of these mistaken directions.[1]

But how can this be accomplished on behalf of our children? How can parents steer a course between the unpleasant alternatives of permissiveness and oppression? What philosophy will guide our efforts?

THE WILL VS. THE SPIRIT

Our objective is not only to shape the will of the child, as described in the previous chapters, *but to do so without breaking his spirit*. To accomplish this purpose we must understand the characteristic difference between the will and the spirit.

As I've stated, a child's *will* is a powerful force in the human personality. It is one of the few intellectual components which arrives full strength at the moment of birth. In a recent issue of *Psychology Today*, this heading described the research findings from a study of infancy: "A baby knows who he is before he has language to tell us so. He reaches deliberately for control of his environment, especially his parents." This scientific disclosure would bring no new revelation to the parents of a strong-willed infant. They have walked the floor with him in the wee small hours, listening to this tiny dictator as he made his wants and wishes abundantly clear.

Later, a defiant toddler can become so angry that he is capable of holding his breath until he loses consciousness. Anyone who has ever witnessed this full measure of willful defiance has been shocked by its power. One headstrong three-year-old recently refused to obey a direct command from her mother, saying, "You're just my *mommy*, you know!"

Another mere mommy wrote me that she found herself in a similar confrontation with her three-year-old son over something that she wanted him to eat. He was so enraged by her insistence that

67

he refused to eat or drink *anything* for two full days. He became weak and lethargic, but steadfastly held his ground. The mother was worried and guilt ridden, as might be expected.

Finally, in desperation, the father looked the child in the eyes and convinced him that he was going to receive a spanking he would never forget if he didn't eat his dinner. With that maneuver, the contest was over. The toddler surrendered. He began to consume everything he could get his hands on, and virtually emptied the refrigerator.

Now tell me, please, why have so few child development authorities recognized this willful defiance? Why have they written so little about it? My guess is that the acknowledgment of childish imperfection would not fit neatly with the humanistic notion that little people are infused with sunshine and goodness, and merely "learn" the meaning of evil. To those who hold that rosy view I can only say, "Take another look!"

The will is not delicate and wobbly. Even for a child in whom the spirit has been sandbagged, there is often a will of steel, making him a threat to himself and others as well. Such a person can sit on a bridge threatening to jump, while the entire army, navy, and local fire department try to save his life.

At the same time, *the will is malleable.* It can and should be molded and polished—not to make a robot of a child for our selfish purposes, but to give him the ability to control his *own* impulses and exercise self-discipline later in life. In fact, we have a God-given responsibility as parents to shape the will in the manner described in the previous chapter.

On the other hand (and let me give this paragraph the strongest possible emphasis), *the spirit of a child is a million times more vulnerable than his will.* It is a delicate flower that can be crushed and broken all too easily (and even unintentionally). The spirit, as I have defined it, relates to the self-esteem or the personal worth that a child feels. It is *the* most fragile characteristic in human nature, being particularly vulnerable to rejection and ridicule and failure.

How, then, are we to shape the will while preserving the spirit intact? It is accomplished by establishing reasonable boundaries and enforcing them with love, but by avoiding any implication that the child is unwanted, unnecessary, foolish, ugly, dumb, a burden, an embarrassment, or a disastrous mistake. Any accusation that assaults the worth of a child in this way can be costly, such as "You are so stupid!" Or, "Why can't you make decent grades in school like your sister?" Or, "You have been a pain in the neck ever since the day you were born!"

THE PROBLEM WITH BILLY

The following letter was sent to me by a mother of three children and illustrates the precise opposite of the principles I am describing. I believe it will be useful to examine this woman's frustrations and the probable causes for her inability to control her defiant son, Billy. (Note: the details of this letter have been changed slightly to conceal the identity of the writer.)

Dear Dr. Dobson:

More than anything else in this world, I want to have a happy family. We have two girls, ages three and five, and a boy who is ten. They don't get along at all. The boy and his father don't get along either. And I find myself screaming at the kids and sitting on my son to keep him from hitting and kicking his sisters.

His teacher of the past year thought he needed to learn better ways of getting along with his classmates. He had some problems on the playground and had a horrible time on the school bus. And he didn't seem to be able to walk from the bus stop to our house without getting in a fight or throwing rocks at somebody. So I usually pick him up and bring him home myself.

He is very bright but writes poorly and hates to do it. He is impulsive and quick tempered (we all are now). He is tall and strong. Our pediatrician says he has "everything going for him." But Billy seldom finds anything constructive to do. He likes to watch television, play in the water and dig in the dirt.

We are very upset about his diet, but haven't been able to do anything about it. He drinks milk and eats Jell-O and crackers and toast. In the past he ate lots of hot dogs and bologna, but not much lately. He also craves chocolate and bubble gum. We have a grandma nearby who sees that he gets lots of it. She also feeds him baby food. We haven't been able to do anything about that, either.

Billy's teachers, the neighbor children and his sisters complain about him swearing and name-calling. This is really an unfortunate situation because we're *always* thinking of him in a bad light. But hardly a day goes by when something isn't upset or broken. He's been breaking windows since he was a toddler. One day in June he came home early from school and found the house locked, so he threw a rock through his bedroom window, broke it, and crawled in. Another day recently he tried the glass cutter on our bedroom mirror. He spends a great deal of time at the grandma's who caters to him. We feel she is a bad influence, but so are we when we're constantly upset and screaming.

Anyhow, we have what seems to be a hopeless situation. He is growing bigger and stronger but not any wiser. So what do we do or where do we go?

My husband says he refuses to take Billy anywhere ever again until he matures and "acts like a civilized human being." He has threatened to put him in a foster home. I couldn't send him to a foster home. He needs people who know what to do with him. Please help us if you can.

Yours truly,

Mrs. T

P.S. Our children are adopted and there isn't much of anything left in our marriage.

This is a very sad plea for help, because the writer is undoubtedly sincere in professing "more than anything else in the world I want to have a happy family." From the tone of her letter, however, it is unlikely that she will *ever* realize her greatest desire. In fact, that specific need for peaceful co-existence and harmony has probably led to many of her problems with Billy. The mother is making two very serious mistakes with her son which are among the most common disciplinary errors.

WHY BILLY'S PARENTS FAILED

First, *Billy's parents have taken no steps to shape his will, although he is begging for their intervention.* It is a terrifying thing to be your own boss at ten years of age—unable to find even one adult who is strong enough to earn your respect. Why else would this lad break every rule and attack every figure of authority? Billy waged war on his teacher at school, but she was baffled by his challenge. All she knew to do was to call his trembling mother and report, "Billy needs to learn better ways of getting along with his classmates." (Didn't she phrase it kindly? You can bet there were some stronger things she could have said about his classroom behavior!)

Billy has been an intolerable brat on the school bus, and he fought with his classmates on the way home, and he broke windows and cut mirrors and used the foulest language and tormented his sisters. He selected the worst possible diet and refused to complete his academic assignments or accept any form of responsibility. Can there be any doubt that Billy was screaming, "Look! I'm doing it all wrong! Doesn't anyone love me enough to care? Can't anyone help me?! I hate the world and the world hates me!"

But Mrs. T's only response to Billy's defiance has been one of utter frustration and distress. She finds herself "screaming at the kids" and "sitting on [her] son" when he misbehaves. Billy is impulsive and quick tempered, but Mrs. T admits "we all are now." Both she and her husband feel grandma is a bad influence, "but so are we when we are constantly upset and screaming." You see, her only "tool" for control is the use of anger and high-pitched wailing and weeping. There is *no* more ineffective approach to child management than this display of volcanic emotion, as we will see in the following chapter.

Clearly Mrs. T and her husband have abdicated their responsibilities to provide *leadership* for their family. Note how many times she says, in essence, *we are powerless to act*. These parents were distressed over Billy's poor diet, "but we haven't been able to do anything about it." Billy's grandmother fed him junk food and bubble gum, but "we haven't been able to do anything about that, either." Likewise, they couldn't stop him from swearing or tormenting his sisters or breaking windows or throwing rocks at his peers.

We who are observing must wonder, why not? Why is the family ship so difficult to steer? Why is it likely to be dashed to pieces on the rocks or run aground on a sandy beach?

The problem is that the ship has no captain! It is drifting aimlessly in the absence of a leader—a decision maker—an authority who could guide it to safer waters.

Now, please note this second error: *instead of*

shaping Billy's rampaging will, as it desperately needed, his parents directed their disciplinary efforts at his damaged spirit.

Not only did they scream and cry and wring their hands in despair, but their frustrations gave rise to personal attacks and hostile rejection. Can't you hear his angry father shouting, "Why don't you grow up and act like a civilized human being instead of an intolerable brat?! Well, I'll tell you something! I'm through with you! I'll never take you anywhere again or even let anyone know that you are my son. As a matter of fact, I'm not sure you are going to *be* my son for very long. If you keep acting like a lawless thug we're going to throw you out of this family—we're going to put you in a foster home. Then we'll see how you like it!"

With each accusation, Billy's self-esteem moved down another notch. But did these personal assaults make him sweeter or more cooperative? Of course not! He just became meaner and more bitter and more convinced of his own worthlessness.

You see, Billy's spirit had been crushed, but his will raged undiminished at hurricane force. And sadly, he is the kind of individual who, as he grows older, often turns his self-hatred on innocent victims outside his family.

HOW TO HANDLE BILLY

If circumstances permitted, it would be my pleasure to have Billy in our home for a period of time. It's not too late to save him and I would feel challenged by the opportunity to try.

How would I approach this defiant youngster? By giving him the following message as soon as his suitcase was unpacked: "Billy, there are several things I want to talk over with you, now that you're a member of our family.

"First, you'll soon learn how much we love you in this house. I'm glad you're here, and I hope these will be the happiest days of your life. And you should know that I care about your feelings and problems and concerns. We invited you here because we wanted you to come, and you will have the same love and respect our own children receive.

"If you have something to say to me, you can

God's Guide to Child-Rearing

Our guiding purpose is to shape the child's will without breaking his spirit. This dual objective is outlined for us throughout the Scriptures, but is specifically stated in two important references.

Shaping the will:
"He [the father] must have proper authority in his own household and be able to control and command the respect of his children" (1 Tim. 3:4, Phillips).

Preserving the spirit:
"And now a word to you parents. Don't keep on scolding and nagging your children, making them angry and resentful. Rather, bring them up with loving discipline the Lord himself approves, with suggestions and godly advice" (Eph. 6:4).

---

come right out and say it. I won't get angry or make you regret expressing yourself. Neither my wife nor I will ever intentionally do anything to hurt you or treat you unkindly. You'll see that these are not just empty promises that you're hearing. This is the way people act when they love each other, and we already love you.

"But, Billy, there are some other things you must also understand. There are going to be some definite rules and acceptable ways to behave in this home, and you are going to have to live within these boundaries just as our other children do. You will carry your share of responsibilities and jobs, and your school work will be given high priority each evening.

"You need to understand, Billy, that my most important job as your guardian is to see that you behave in ways that are healthy to yourself and others. It may take you a week or two to adjust to this new situation, but you're going to make it and I'm going to be here to help you. And when you refuse to obey, I will punish you immediately. This will help you change some of the harmful, destructive ways you've learned to behave. But even when I must discipline you, I will love you as much as I do right now."

The first time Billy disobeyed what he knew to be my definite instructions, I would react decisively. There would be no screaming or derogatory accusations, although he would soon know that I meant what I had said. He would probably be given a stiff spanking and sent to bed an hour or two early. The following morning we would discuss the issue rationally, reassure him of our continuing love, and then start over. Most delinquent children respond beautifully to this one-two punch of love and consistent discipline. It's an unbeatable combination!

CHAPTER
5

*The Common Error—
and How to Avoid It*

The most common error in disciplining children,
and perhaps the most costly, is the *inappropriate
use of anger* in attempting to control boys or girls.

There is no more ineffective method of leading human beings (of all ages) than the use of
irritation and anger. Nevertheless, *most* adults
rely primarily on their own emotional response
to secure the cooperation of children.

One teacher said on a national television program, "I like being a professional educator, but I
hate the daily task of teaching. My children are
so unruly that I have to stay mad at them all the
time just to control the classroom." How utterly
frustrating to be required to be mean and angry
as part of a routine assignment, year in and year
out. Yet many teachers (and parents) know of
no other way to lead children. Believe me, it is
exhausting and it doesn't work!

Consider your *own* motivational system. Suppose you are driving your automobile home from work this evening, and you exceed the speed limit by forty miles per hour. Standing on a street corner is a lone policeman who has not been given the means to arrest you. He has no squad car or motorcycle; he wears no badge, carries no gun, and can write no tickets. All he is commissioned to do is stand on the curb and scream insults as you speed past. Would you slow down just because he shakes his fist in protest? Of course not! You might wave to him as you streak by. His anger would achieve little except to make him appear comical and foolish.

On the other hand, nothing influences the way Mr. Motorist drives more than occasionally seeing in the rear view mirror a black and white vehicle in hot pursuit with nineteen red lights flashing. When his car is brought to a stop, a dignified, courteous patrolman approaches the driver's window. He is six foot nine, has a voice like the Lone Ranger, and carries a sawed-off shotgun on each hip. "Sir," he says firmly but politely, "our radar unit indicates you were traveling sixty-five miles per hour in a twenty-five-mile zone. May I see your driver's license, please?" He opens his leather-bound book of citations and leans toward you.

He has revealed no hostility and offers no criticisms, yet you immediately go to pieces. You fumble nervously to locate the small document in your wallet (the one with the horrible Polaroid picture). Why are your hands moist and your mouth dry? Why is your heart thumping in your throat? Because the course of *action* that John Law is about to take is notoriously unpleasant. Alas, it is his *action* which dramatically affects your future driving habits.

WHY ANGER DOESN'T WORK

Disciplinary action influences behavior; anger does not. As a matter of fact, I am convinced that adult anger produces a destructive kind of disrespect in the minds of our children. They perceive that our frustration is caused by our inability to control the situation. We represent justice to them, yet we're on the verge of tears as we flail the air with our hands and shout empty threats and warnings.

Let me ask: Would *you* respect a superior court judge who behaved that emotionally in administering legal justice? Certainly not. This is why the judicial system is carefully controlled to appear objective, rational, and dignified.

I am not recommending that parents and teachers conceal their legitimate emotions from their children. I am not suggesting that we be like bland and unresponsive robots who hold everything inside. There are times when our boys and girls become insulting or disobedient and our irritation is entirely appropriate. In fact, it *should* be revealed, or else we appear phony and unreal.

My point is merely that anger often becomes a *tool* used consciously for the purpose of influencing behavior. It is ineffective and can be damaging to the relationship between generations.

HENRY'S STORY

Let's look at a specific illustration that could represent any one of 20 million homes this afternoon. Henry is in the second grade and arrives home from school in a whirlwind of activity. He has been wiggling and giggling since he awakened this morning, but incredibly, he still has excess energy to burn. His mother, Mrs. Geritol, is not in the same condition. She has been on her feet since staggering out of bed at 6:30 A.M. She fixed breakfast for the family, cleaned the mess, got Dad off to work, and sent Henry to school, and then settled into a long day trying to keep her twin toddlers from killing themselves. By the time Henry blows in from school, she has put in eight hours' work without a rest. (Toddlers don't take breaks, so why should their mothers?)

Despite Mom's fatigue, she can hardly call it a day. She still has at least six hours of work left to do, including going to the grocery store, fixing the evening meal, washing the dishes, giving the twins their baths, putting on their diapers, tucking them in bed, helping Henry with his homework, joining in his prayers, brushing his teeth, reading him a story, saying good-night, and then bringing him four glasses of water throughout the closing forty-five minutes of the evening. I get depressed just thinking about the weary Mrs. Geritol and her domestic duties.

Henry is not so sympathetic, however, and arrives home from school in a decidedly mischievous mood. He can't find anything interesting to do, so he begins to irritate his uptight mother.

He teases one of the twins to the point of tears, and pulls the cat's tail, and spills the dog's water.

Mother is nagging by this time, but Henry acts like he doesn't hear her. Then he goes to the toy closet and begins jerking out games and boxes of plastic toys and Pickup Stix. Mom knows that someone is going to have to clean up all that mess and she has a vague notion about who will get the assignment. The intensity of her voice is rising again. She orders him to the bathroom to wash his hands in preparation for dinner. Henry is gone for fifteen minutes, and when he returns his hands are still dirty. Mom's pulse is pounding through her veins by this time, and there is a definite migraine sensation above her left eye.

Finally, the day wears down to its concluding responsibility: Henry's bedtime. But Henry does not *want* to go to bed and he knows it will take his harassed mother at least thirty minutes to get him there. Henry does not do *anything* against his wishes unless his mother becomes very angry and "blows up" at him. Mrs. Geritol begins the emotional process of coercing her reluctant son to take his bath and prepare for bed. This portion of the story was included in *The New Dare to Discipline*, and we will quote from that description:[1]

> Henry is sitting on the floor, playing with his games. Mom looks at her watch and says, "Henry, it's nearly nine o'clock (a thirty-minute exaggeration), so gather up your toys and go take your bath." Now Henry and Mom both know that she didn't mean for him to *immediately* take a bath. She merely wanted him to start

thinking about taking his bath. She would have fainted dead away if he had responded to her empty command.

Approximately ten minutes later, Mom speaks again. "Now, Henry, it's getting later and you have school tomorrow; I want those toys picked up and then I want you in that tub!" She still does not intend for Henry to obey, and he knows it. Her *real* message is, "We're getting closer, Hank." Henry shuffles around and stacks a box or two to demonstrate that he heard her. Then he settles down for a few more minutes of play.

Six minutes pass and Mom issues another command, this time with more passion and threat in her voice, "Now listen, young man, I told you to get a move on, and I meant it!" To Henry, this means he must get his toys picked up and m-e-a-n-d-e-r toward the bathroom door. If his mother rapidly pursues him, then he must carry out the assignment posthaste. However, if Mom's mind wanders before she performs the last step of this ritual, or if the phone miraculously rings, Henry is free to enjoy a few minutes' reprieve.

You see, Henry and his mother are involved in a familiar one-act play. They both know the rules and the role being enacted by the opposite actor. The entire scene is preprogrammed, computerized, and scripted. In actuality, it's a virtual replay of a scene that occurs night after night. Whenever Mom wants Henry to do something he dislikes, she progresses through graduated steps of phony anger, beginning with calmness and ending with a red flush and threats. Henry does not have to move until she reaches her flashpoint.

How foolish this game is. Since Mom controls Hank with empty threats, she must stay half-irritated all the time. Her relationship with her children is contaminated, and she ends each day with a pulsing migraine above her left eye. She can never count on instant obedience, because it takes her at least five minutes to work up a believable degree of anger.

How much better it is to use *action* to achieve the desired behavior. There are hundreds of approaches that will bring a desired response, some of which involve slight pain, while others offer the child a reward. The use of rewards or "positive reinforcement" . . . will not be presented here. But minor pain or "negative reinforcement" can also provide excellent motivation for the child.

When a parent's calm request for obedience is ignored by a child, Mom or Dad should have some means of making their youngster *want* to cooperate. For those who can think of no such device, I will suggest one: it is the muscle lying snugly against the base of the neck. Anatomy books list it as the trapezius muscle, and when firmly squeezed, it sends little messengers to the brain saying, "This hurts: avoid recurrence at all costs." The pain is only temporary; it can cause no damage. But it is an amazingly effective and practical recourse for parents when their youngster ignores a direct command to move.

Let's return to the bedtime scene with Henry, and let me suggest how it could be replayed more effectively. To begin, his mother should have forewarned him that he had fifteen more minutes to play. No one, child or adult, likes a sudden interruption of his activity. It then would have been wise to set the alarm clock or the stove buzzer. When the fifteen minutes passed and the buzzer sounded, Mom should have quietly told Henry to go take his bath. If he didn't move immediately, his shoulder muscle could have been squeezed. If Henry learns that this procedure or some other unpleasantry is invariably visited upon him, he will move before the consequences ensue.

I know that some of my readers could argue that the deliberate, premeditated application of minor pain to a small child is a harsh and unloving thing to do. To others, it will seem like pure barbarism. I obviously disagree. Given a choice between a harassed, screaming, threatening mother who blows up several times a day versus a mom who has a reasonable, controlled response to disobedience, I would certainly recommend the latter. In the long run, the quieter home is better for Johnny, too, because of the avoidance of strife between generations.

On the other hand, when a youngster discovers there is no threat behind the millions of words he hears, he stops listening to them. The only messages he responds to are those reaching a peak of emotion, which means there is much screaming and yelling going on. The child is pulling in the opposite direction, fraying Mom's nerves and straining the parent-child relationship. But the most important limitation of those verbal reprimands is that their user often has to resort to physical punishment in the end anyway. It is also more likely to be severe, because the adult is irritated and out of control. Thus, instead of the discipline being administered in a calm and judicious manner, the parent has become unnerved and frustrated, swinging wildly at the belligerent child. There was no reason for a fight to have occurred. The situation could have ended very differently if the parental attitude had been one of confident serenity.

Speaking softly, almost pleasantly, Mom says, "Henry, you know what happens when you don't mind me; now I don't see any reason in the world why I should have to make you uncomfortable just to get your cooperation tonight, but if you insist, I'll play the game with you. When the buzzer sounds you let me know what the decision is."

The child then has the choice to make, and the advantages to him of obeying his mother's wishes are clear. She need not scream. She need not threaten to shorten his life. She need not become upset. She is in command. Of course, Mother will have to prove two or three times that she will apply the pain or other punishment, if necessary. Occasionally throughout the coming months, Henry will check to see if she is still at the helm. That question is easily answered.

DIAGRAM OF A CLASH

An understanding of the interaction between Henry and his mother can be very helpful to parents who have become "screamers" and don't know why. Let's look at their relationship during that difficult evening as diagrammed on the accompanying chart. Note that Henry's mother greeted him at the front door after school, which represented a low point of irritation. From that time forward, however, her emotion built and intensified until it reached a moment of explosion at the end of the day.

By her ultimate display of anger at bedtime, Mrs. Geritol made it clear to Henry that she was through warning and was now ready to take definite action. You see, most parents (even those who are very permissive) have a point on the scale beyond which they will not be pushed; inevitable punishment looms immediately across that line.

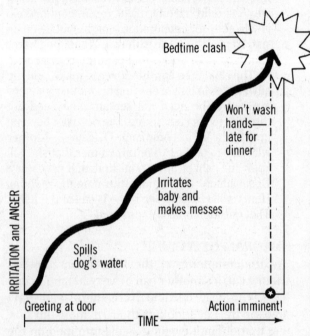

HOW KIDS SHOW SAVVY

The amazing thing about children is that they know *precisely* where their parents typically draw the line. We adults reveal our particular points of action to them in at least a dozen subtle ways.

Only at those moments do we use their middle names ("William Thornton Langford, get in the tub!"). Our speech also becomes more staccato and abrupt ("Young! Man! I! Told! You! . . ."). Our faces turn red (an important clue). We jump from our chairs. And Junior knows it is time to cooperate.

The other interesting thing about children is that having identified the circumstances which immediately precede disciplinary action, they will take their parents directly to that barrier and bump it repeatedly, but will *seldom* go beyond it deliberately.

Once or twice Henry will ignore his mother's emotional fireworks, just to see if she has the courage to deliver on her promise. When that question has been answered, he will do what she demands in the nick of time to avoid punishment.

THE BIG TRUTH ABOUT ANGER
Now this brings us to the punch line of this important discussion. I must admit that what I am about to write is difficult to express and may not be fully understood by my readers. It can, however, be of value to parents who want to stop fighting with their children.

I have said that parental anger often signals to Junior that he has reached his action line. Therefore, he obeys, albeit reluctantly, only when Mom or Dad "get mad," indicating that they will now resort to punishment.

On the other hand, the parents observe that Junior's surrender occurs simultaneously with their anger and inaccurately conclude that their emotional explosion is what forced him to yield. Thus, their anger seems necessary for control in the future. They have grossly misunderstood the situation.

Returning to the story of Henry, his mother told him six or eight times to take his bath. Only when she "blew up" did he get in the tub, leading her to believe that her anger produced his obedience. She was wrong! It was not her anger that sent Hank to the suds—it was the *action* he believed to be imminent. Her anger was nothing more than a tip-off that Mom was frustrated enough to spank his pink bottom. Henry *cares* about that!

I have written this entire chapter in order to convey this one message: you don't *need* anger to control children. You *do* need action, occasionally. Furthermore, you can apply the action anywhere on the time line that is convenient, and children will live contentedly within that boundary.

In fact, the closer the action moves to the front of the conflict the less punishment is required. A pinch of the trapezius muscle would not be a sufficient deterrent at the end of a two-hour struggle, whereas it is more than adequate when the conflict is minimal. (Incidentally, I do not recommend that mothers weighing less than ninety pounds try to squeeze the shoulder muscles of their big teenagers. There are definite risks involved in that procedure. The general rule to follow is, "If you can't reach it, don't squeeze it.")

THE BEST TIME FOR ACTION

Let me return to Dr. Spock's valuable observation, particularly as it applies to the diagram. "Parental submissiveness [by that he refers to parents who have *no action line,* or else it occurs too late] doesn't avoid unpleasantness; it makes it inevitable." (If you don't take a stand early, a child is *compelled* by his nature to push you further.) The child's defiance, then, "makes the parent increasingly more resentful, until it finally explodes in a display of anger." That is precisely what I have been attempting to say for the past twenty years!

Contained in this statement is an understanding of children which some adults grasp intuitively, while others never quite "feel it." It involves the delicate balance between love and control, recognizing that a reasonable and consistent action line does not assault self-worth, but represents a source of security for an immature child.

Fathers often comprehend this principle better than mothers, for reasons which escape me. Thus, it is very common for a mother to say to me: "I don't understand my kids. They will do exactly what their father demands, but they won't mind me at all." The behavior of her children is no mystery. They are bright enough to notice that Dad draws his action line *earlier* than Mother. She screams and argues, while he quietly acts.

Children often understand these forces even better than their parents, who are bogged down with adult responsibilities and worries. That is why so many kids are able to win the contest of wills; they devote their *primary* effort to the game, while we grown-ups play only when we must.

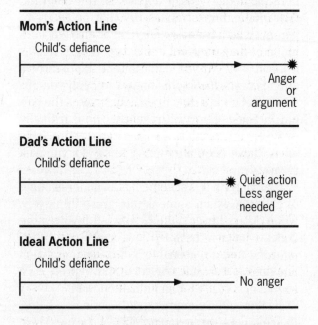

Mom's Action Line

Child's defiance

Anger or argument

Dad's Action Line

Child's defiance

Quiet action
Less anger
needed

Ideal Action Line

Child's defiance

No anger

One father overheard his five-year-old daughter, Laura, say to her little sister who was doing something wrong, "Mmmm, I'm going to tell Mommy on you. No! I'll tell Daddy. He's worse!" Laura had evaluated the disciplinary measures of her two parents, and concluded that one was more effective than the other.

This same child was observed by her father to have become especially disobedient and defiant. She was irritating other family members and looking for ways to avoid minding her parents.

Her dad decided not to confront her directly about this change in behavior, but to punish her consistently for every offense until she settled down. Thus, for three or four days, he let Laura get away with nothing. She was spanked, stood in the corner, and sent to her bedroom.

At the conclusion of the fourth day, she was sitting on the bed with her father and younger sister. Without provocation, Laura pulled the hair of the toddler who was looking at a book. Her dad promptly thumped her on the head with his large hand. Laura did not cry, but sat in silence for a moment or two, and then said, "Hurrummph! All my tricks are not working!"

CAN YOUR CHILD MANIPULATE YOU?

If the reader will recall his own childhood years, he will probably remember similar events in which the disciplinary techniques of adults were analyzed consciously and their weaknesses probed.

When I was a child, I once spent the night with a rambunctious friend who seemed to know every move his parents were going to make. Earl was like a military general who had deciphered the enemy code, permitting him to outmaneuver his opponents at every turn. After we were tucked into our own twin beds that night, he gave me an astounding description of his father's temper.

Earl said, "When my dad gets very angry, he uses some really bad words that will amaze you." (He listed three or four startling examples from past experience.)

I replied, "I don't believe it!"

Mr. Walker was a very tall, reserved man who seemed to have it all together. I just couldn't conceive of his saying the words Earl had quoted.

"Want me to prove it to you?" said Earl mischievously. "All we have to do is keep on laughing and talking instead of going to sleep. My dad will come and tell us to be quiet over and over, and he'll get madder and madder every time he has to settle us down. Then you'll hear his cuss words. Just wait and see."

I was a bit dubious about this plan, but I did want to see the dignified Mr. Walker at his profane best. So Earl and I kept his poor father running back and forth like a yo-yo for over an hour. And as predicted, he became more intense and hostile each time he returned to our bedroom. I was getting very nervous and would have called off the demonstration, but Earl had been through it all before. He kept telling me, "It won't be long now."

Finally, about midnight, it happened. Mr. Walker's patience expired. He came thundering down the hall toward our room, shaking the entire house as his feet pounded the floor. He burst through the bedroom door and leaped on Earl's bed, flailing at the boy who was safely buried beneath three or four layers of blankets. Then from his lips came a stream of words that had seldom reached my tender ears. I was shocked, but Earl was delighted.

Even while his father was whacking the covers with his hand and screaming his profanity, Earl raised up and shouted to me, "Did-ja hear 'em? Huh? Didn't I tell ya? I tolja he would say it!" It's a wonder that Mr. Walker didn't kill his son at that moment!

I lay awake that night thinking about the episode and made up my mind *never* to let a child manipulate me like that when I grew up. Don't you see how important disciplinary techniques are to a child's respect for his parents? When a forty-five-pound bundle of trouble can deliberately reduce his powerful mother or father to a trembling, snarling mass of frustrations, then something changes in their relationship. Something precious is lost. The child develops an attitude of contempt which is certain to erupt during the stormy adolescent years to come. I sincerely wish every adult understood that simple characteristic of human nature.

TWO MEN WHO UNDERSTOOD KIDS

Near my home in Arcadia, California, is a tan gentleman who certainly understands the way children think. He owns and operates Bud Lyndon's Swim School. Mr. Lyndon must be approaching sixty years of age now, and he has been working with youngsters most of his life. He has a remarkable comprehension of the principles of discipline, and I enjoy sitting at poolside just to watch the man work.

However, there are few child developmentalists who could explain why he is so successful with the little swimmers in his pool. He is not soft and delicate in his manner; in fact, he tends to be somewhat gruff. When the kids get out of line he splashes water in their faces and says sternly, "Who told you to move? Stay where I put you until I ask you to swim!" He calls the boys "Men of Tomorrow," and other pet names. His class is regimented and every minute is utilized purposefully.

But would you believe it, the children *love* Bud Lyndon. Why? Because they know that he loves them.

Within his gruff manner is a message of affection that might escape the adult observer. Mr. Lyndon never embarrasses a child intentionally, and he "covers" for the youngster who swims more poorly. He delicately balances his authority with a subtle affection that attracts children like the Pied Piper. Mr. Bud Lyndon understands the meaning of discipline with love.

When I was in the ninth grade I had an athletic coach who affected me the same way. He was the master of the moment, and no one *dared* challenge his authority. I would have fought wild lions before tackling Mr. Ayers.

Yes, I feared him. We all did. But he never abused his power. He treated me courteously and respectfully at a time when I needed all of the dignity I could get. Combined with his acceptance of the individual was an obvious self-confidence and ability to lead a pack of adolescent wolves who had devoured less capable teachers. And that's why my ninth-grade gym coach had a greater influence on me than any other person during my fifteenth year. Mr. Craig Ayers understood discipline with love.

Not every parent can be like Mr. Lyndon or Mr. Ayers, and I would not suggest that they try. Nor would it be wise for a mother to display the same gruffiness at home that is appropriate on the athletic field or at the pool. Each person must fit his approach to discipline within his own personality patterns and the responses that feel natural.

However, the overriding principle remains the same for men and women, mothers and fathers, coaches and teachers, pediatricians and psychologists. It involves:

- discipline with love
- a reasonable introduction to responsibility and self-control
- parental leadership with a minimum of anger
- respect for the dignity and worth of the child
- realistic boundaries that are enforced with confident firmness
- a judicious use of rewards and punishment to those who challenge and resist.

It is a system that bears the approval of the Creator Himself.

CHAPTER
6

Why Professionals Don't Always Know Best

When a child was born during the 1800s or before, his inexperienced mother was assisted by many friends and relatives who hovered around to offer their advice and support.

Very few of these aunts and grandmothers and neighbors had ever read a book on child rearing, but that was no handicap. They possessed a certain folk wisdom which gave them confidence in handling babies and children. They had a prescribed answer for every situation, whether it proved to be right or wrong. Thus, a young woman was systematically taught how to "mother" by older women who had many years' experience in caring for little people.

With the disappearance of this "extended family," however, the job of motherhood became more frightening. Many young couples today do not have access to such supportive relatives and friends. They live in a mobile society wherein the next-door neighbors are often total strangers.

Furthermore, their own mothers and fathers may live in faraway Detroit or Dallas or Portland (and might not be trusted even if they were available to help).

Consequently, young parents often experience great anxieties over their lack of preparation for raising children. Dr. Benjamin Spock described their fears in this way: "I can remember mothers who cried on the morning they were to take their baby home. 'I won't know what to do,' they wailed."

THE ROOTS OF
PROFESSIONAL PARENTING

This anxiety has brought parents rushing to the "experts" for information and advice. They have turned to pediatricians, psychologists, psychiatrists, and educators for answers to their questions about the complexities of parenthood.

Therefore, increasing numbers of American children have been reared according to this professional consultation during the past forty years. In fact, no country on earth has embraced the teachings of child psychology and the offerings of family specialists more than has the United States.

It is now appropriate that we ask, "What has been the effect of this professional influence?" One would expect that the mental health of our children would exceed that of individuals raised in nations not having this technical assistance.

Such has not been the case. Juvenile delinquency, drug abuse, alcoholism, unwanted pregnancies, mental illness, and suicide are rampant among the young and continue their steady rise.

In many ways, we have made a mess of parenthood! Of course, I would not be so naive as to blame all these woes on the bad advice of the "experts," but I believe they have played a role in creating the problem. Why? *Because in general, behavioral scientists have lacked confidence in the Judeo-Christian ethic and have disregarded the wisdom of this priceless tradition!*

It appears to me that the twentieth century has spawned a generation of professionals who felt qualified to ignore the parental attitudes and practices of more than 2,000 years, substituting instead their own wobbly-legged insights of the moment. Each authority, writing from his own limited experience and reflecting his own unique biases, has sold us his guesses and suppositions as though they represented Truth itself.

One anthropologist, for example, wrote an incredibly gallish article in *The Saturday Evening Post*, November 1968, entitled "We Scientists Have a Right to Play God." Dr. Edmund Leach stated,

> There can be no source for these moral judgments except the scientist himself. In traditional religion, morality was held to derive from God, but God was only credited with the authority to establish and enforce moral rules because He was also credited with supernatural powers of creation and destruction. Those powers have now been usurped by man, and he must take on the moral responsibility that goes with them.[1]

That paragraph summarizes the many ills of our day. Arrogant men like Edmund Leach have argued God out of existence and put themselves in His exalted place. Armed with that authority, they have issued their ridiculous opinions to the public with unflinching confidence. In turn, desperate families grabbed their porous recommendations like life preservers, which often sank to the bottom, taking their passengers down with them.

MORAL RELATIVISM AND THE HOME

These false teachings have included the notions that loving discipline is damaging, and irresponsibility is healthy, and religious instruction is hazardous, and defiance is a valuable ventilator of anger, and all authority is dangerous, and on and on it goes. In more recent years, this humanistic perspective has become even more extreme and anti-Christian.

For example, one mother told me recently that she works in a youth project which has obtained the consultative services of a certain psychologist. He has been teaching the parents of kids in the program that in order for young girls to grow up with more healthy attitudes toward sexuality, their fathers should have intercourse with them when they are twelve years of age.

If you gasped at that suggestion, be assured that it shocked me also. Yet this is where moral relativism leads—this is the ultimate product of a human endeavor which accepts no standards, honors no cultural values, acknowledges no absolutes, and serves no "god" except the human mind. King Solomon wrote about such foolish efforts in Proverbs 14:12 (KJV): "There is a way which *seemeth* right unto a man, but the end thereof are the ways of death."

THE CREATOR'S PRESCRIPTION FOR PARENTS TODAY

Now admittedly, the book you have been reading contains many suggestions and perspectives which I have not attempted to validate or prove. How do my writings differ from the unsupported recommendations of those whom I have criticized?

The distinction lies in the *source* of the views being presented. The underlying principles expressed herein are not my own innovative insights which would be forgotten in a brief season or two. Instead, they originated with the inspired biblical writers who gave us the foundation for all relationships in the home.

As such, these principles have been handed down generation after generation to this very day. Our ancestors taught them to their children who taught them to their children, keeping the knowledge alive for posterity. Now, unfortunately, that understanding is being vigorously challenged in some circles and altogether forgotten in others.

If I have had a primary mission in writing this book, therefore, it has not been to earn royalty or propagate the name of James Dobson or demonstrate my professional skills. My purpose has been nothing more ambitious than to verbalize the Judeo-Christian tradition regarding discipline of children and to apply those concepts to today's families.

This approach has been deeply engrained in the Western culture but has never been expressly written, to my knowledge. It involves:

- control with love
- a reasonable introduction to self-discipline and responsibility
- parental *leadership* which seeks the best interest of the child
- respect for the dignity and worth of every member of the family
- realistic boundaries that are enforced with confident firmness
- a judicious use of rewards and punishment when required for training

It is a system that has existed for more than twenty centuries of parenthood. I did not invent it, nor can I change it. My task has been merely to report what I believe to be the prescription of the Creator Himself.

And I am convinced that this understanding will remain viable for as long as mothers and fathers and children cohabit the face of the earth. It will certainly outlive humanism and the puny efforts of mankind to find an alternative.

QUESTIONS AND ANSWERS

My three-year-old daughter, Nancy, plays unpleasant games with me in grocery stores. She runs when I call her and makes demands for candy and gum and cupcakes. When I refuse, she throws the most embarrassing temper tantrums you can imagine. I don't want to punish her in front of all those people and she knows it. What should I do?

If there are sanctuaries where the usual rules and restrictions do not apply, then your children will behave differently in those protected zones than elsewhere. I would suggest that you have a talk with Nancy on the next trip to the market. Tell her exactly what you expect, and make it clear that you mean business. Then when the same behavior occurs, take her to the car or behind the building and do what you would have done at home. She'll get the message.

My ten-year-old often puts his milk glass too close to his elbow when eating, and has

knocked it over at least six times. I keep telling him to move the glass, but he won't listen. When he spilt the milk again yesterday, I jerked him up and gave him a spanking with a belt. Today I don't feel good about the incident. Should I have reacted more patiently?

It is all too easy to tell a mother she shouldn't have become so upset over something that happened yesterday. After all, I'm not the one who had to clean up the mess. However, your son did not *intend* to spill his milk and he was, in effect, punished for his irresponsibility. It would have been better to create a method of grabbing his attention and helping him remember to return his glass to a safe area.

For example, you could have cut an "off limits" zone from red construction paper, and taped it to the side of his plate. If Junior placed his glass on that paper, he would have to help wash the dishes after the evening meal. I guarantee you that he would seldom "forget" again. In fact, this procedure would probably sensitize him to the location of the glass, even after the paper was removed.

How can I know for sure if my child is deliberately disobeying me?

That question has been asked of me hundreds of times. A mother will say, "I think Chuckie was being disrespectful when I told him to take his bath, but I'm not sure what he was thinking."

There is a very straightforward solution to this parental dilemma: use the first occasion for the purpose of clarifying the next. Say to your son,

"Chuck, your answer to me just now sounded sassy. I'm not sure how you intended it. But so we will understand each other, don't talk to me like that again." If it occurs again, you'll know it was deliberate.

Most confusion over how to discipline results from parents' failure to define the limits properly. If you're hazy on what is acceptable and unacceptable, then your child will be doubly confused. Therefore, don't punish until you have drawn the boundaries too clearly to be missed. Most children will then accept them with only an occasional indiscretion.

How do you get children to behave politely and responsibly, especially when they pay no attention to your repeated instructions?

Kids love games of all sorts, especially if adults will get involved with them. It is often possible to turn a teaching situation into a fun activity which "sensitizes" the entire family to the issue you're trying to teach.

If you'll pardon yet another personal example, let me tell you how we taught our children to put their napkins in their laps before eating. We tried reminding them for two or three years, but simply weren't getting through. Then we turned it into a family game.

Now, if one of the Dobsons takes a single bit of food before putting his napkin in his lap, he is required to go to his bedroom and count to twenty-five in a loud voice. This game is highly effective, although it has some definite disadvantages. You can't imagine how foolish Shirley and I feel when we're standing in an empty section of the house, counting to twenty-five while our kids giggle. Ryan, particularly, *never* forgets his napkin and he loves to catch the rest of us in a moment of preoccupation. He will sit perfectly still, looking straight ahead until the first bite of food goes in. Then he wheels toward the offender, points his finger, and says, "Gotcha!!"

For all of those many teaching objectives that involve teaching responsibility (rather than conquering willful defiance), game-playing should be considered as the method of choice.

Should my child be permitted to say, "I hate you!" when he is angry?

Not in my opinion. Other writers will tell you that all children hate their parents occasionally and should be permitted to ventilate that hostility. I believe it is possible (and far more healthy) to encourage the expression of negative feelings without reinforcing temper tantrums and violent behavior.

If my child screamed his hatred at me *for the first time* in a moment of red-faced anger, I would probably wait until his passion had cooled and then convey the following message in a loving, sincere manner: "Charlie, I know you were very upset earlier today when we had our disagreement, and I think we should talk about what you were feeling. *All* children get angry at their parents now and then, especially when they feel unfairly treated.

"I understand your frustration and I'm sorry we got into such a hassle. But that does not excuse you for saying, 'I hate you!' You'll learn that no matter how upset I become over something you've done, I'll *never* tell you that I hate you. And I can't permit you to talk that way to me.

"When people love each other, as you and I do, they don't want to hurt one another. It hurt me for you to say that you hated me, just as you would be hurt if I said something like that to you. You can, however, tell me what angers you, and I will listen carefully.

"If I am wrong, I will do my best to change the things you dislike. So I want you to understand that you are free to say *anything* you wish to me as always, even if your feelings are not very pleasant.

"But you will never be permitted to scream and call names and throw temper tantrums. If you behave in those childish ways, I will have to punish you as I would a little child.

"Is there anything you need to say to me now? (If not, then put your arms around my neck because I love you!)"

My purpose would be to permit the ventilation of negative feelings without encouraging violent, disrespectful, manipulative behavior.

Would you, then, go so far as to apologize to a child if you felt you had been in the wrong?

I certainly would—and indeed, I have. A few years ago I was burdened with pressing responsibilities which made me fatigued and irritable.

One particular evening I was especially grouchy and short-tempered with my ten-year-old daughter. I knew I was not being fair, but was simply too tired to correct my manner. Through the course of the evening, I blamed Danae for things that were not her fault and upset her needlessly several times.

After going to bed, I felt bad about the way I had behaved and I decided to apologize the next morning. After a good night of sleep and a tasty breakfast, I felt much more optimistic about life. I approached my daughter before she left for school and said, "Danae, I'm sure you know that daddies are not perfect human beings. We get tired and irritable just like other people, and there are times when we are not proud of the way we behave. I know that I wasn't fair with you last night. I was terribly grouchy, and I want you to forgive me."

Danae put her arms around me and shocked me down to my toes. She said, "I knew you were going to have to apologize, Daddy, and it's okay; I forgive you."

Can there be any doubt that children are often more aware of the struggles between generations than are their busy, harassed parents?

NOTES

CHAPTER 2
1. John Valusek, *Parade Magazine*, February 6, 1977, n.p.
2. Dr. James C. Dobson, *Hide or Seek* (Old Tappan, N.J.: Fleming H. Revell Company, 1974), n.p. Used by permission.

CHAPTER 3
1. T. Berry Brazelton, *Toddlers and Parents: A Declaration of Independence* (New York: Delacorte Press, 1974), pp. 101–110.
2. From the *APA Monitor* (published by the American Psychological Association, Washington, D.C.), Vol. 7, No. 4, 1976, n.p.
3. Dr. Luther Woodward, in *Your Child from Two to Five*, Morton Edwards, editor (New York: Permabooks, 1955), pp. 95, 96.
4. Dr. James Dobson, *The New Dare to Discipline* (Carol Stream, Ill.: Tyndale House Publishers, 2008), pp. 14–15.

CHAPTER 4
1. Marguerite and Willard Beecher, *Parents on the Run: A Commonsense Book for Today's Parents* (New York: Crown Publishers, Inc., © 1955 by Marguerite and Willard Beecher), pp. 6–8. Used by permission of Crown Publishers, Inc.

CHAPTER 5
1. Dobson, *The New Dare to Discipline*, pp. 37–40.

CHAPTER 6
1. Dr. Edmund Leach, "We Scientists Have a Right to Play God," *The Saturday Evening Post*, November 1968. ©1968 The Curtis Publishing Company, Indianapolis, Ind.

ABOUT THE AUTHOR

James C. Dobson, Ph.D., hosts the daily radio program *Dr. James Dobson's Family Talk*. A licensed psychologist and marriage, family, and child counselor, he is a clinical member of the American Association for Marriage and Family Therapy. For 14 years Dr. Dobson was an associate clinical professor of pediatrics at the University of Southern California School of Medicine, and he served for 17 years on the attending staff of Childrens Hospital Los Angeles in the Division of Child Development and Medical Genetics. He earned a Ph.D. from the University of Southern California (1967) in the field of child development. He is the author of more than 30 books, including *The New Strong-Willed Child*, *When God Doesn't Make Sense*, *Night Light*, *Bringing Up Boys*, and the *New York Times* bestseller *Bringing Up Girls*. He was elected in 2008 to the National Radio Hall of Fame. Dr. Dobson is married to Shirley and is the father of two grown children, Danae and Ryan, and the grandfather of Lincoln and Luci Rose. He resides in Colorado.

James C. Dobson

Tune in to
Dr. James Dobson's Family Talk.

To learn more about
Dr. James Dobson's Family Talk
or to find a station in your area,
visit www.drjamesdobson.org
or call (877) 732-6825.

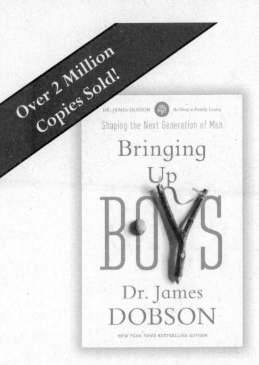

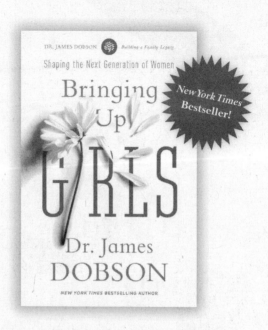

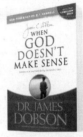
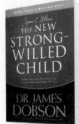

LOVE MUST BE TOUGH
978-1-4143-1745-8 (softcover)

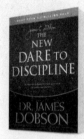

THE NEW DARE TO DISCIPLINE
978-0-8423-0506-8 (softcover)

LIFE ON THE EDGE
978-1-4143-1744-1 (softcover)